THEN AND NOW

THEN AND NOW

THE HISTORIC CHURCH AND THE
YOUNGER CHURCHES

BY

JOHN FOSTER

Professor of Church History in the
Selly Oak Colleges, Birmingham
Author of *Chinese Realities*,
The Chinese Church in Action,
I Believe,
The Church of the T'ang Dynasty, etc.

STUDENT CHRISTIAN MOVEMENT PRESS
58 BLOOMSBURY STREET, LONDON, W.C.1

First published January 1942

Distributed in Canada by our exclusive agents
The Macmillan Company of Canada Ltd.
70 Bond Street, Toronto

PRINTED IN GREAT BRITAIN BY
NORTHUMBERLAND PRESS LIMITED
GATESHEAD ON TYNE

CONTENTS

To

W. F. LOFTHOUSE

ὦ φίλη Κεφαλή, . . .
σώσας μὲν παρόντας τοῖς ἱεροῖς σου μαθήμασι,
σώζων δὲ ταῖς εὐχαῖς καὶ ἀποδημήσαντας.

'Beloved Head,
Who didst save us when present at thy holy lessons,
Who dost save us by thy prayers even when gone abroad.'
(Gregory Thaumaturgus, *Address to Origen*, xix.)

INTRODUCTION

DURING the last war I had a shipmate who used to get stuck in his reading at any but the most usual words. You would hear him—for like many simple people he read best aloud—with the newspaper: 'To-day a bill was passed by Par—Parl—some so-and-so thing!' With that ejaculation he always seemed ready to proceed as though there had been no interruption to the sense.

Readers of this book must feel free to skip a bit, though without the need of a swear-word. For one of my hopes is that those to whom the history of the Church is a new subject may here, so far from being overawed by unfamiliar things, find an appetite for more. I have also had in mind the student to whom historical references will be a recall to familiar and beloved ground. I have even ventured to hope that some teachers of theological subjects might discover, if not (as a too-kind editor described my work[1]) 'the new presentation of Church History', at any rate a new background to their own teaching. I find encouragement for this sort of contribution in some words of one who has made wise criticisms of our British universities: 'One might even say that part of the difficulties which have arisen in the educational sphere is due to over-emphasis on research in fields

---

[1] *Expository Times*, LII, 46.

where *the handling of existing knowledge and material is no less important than the exploration of new regions.*'[1]

Part of the book grew out of lectures given to a group of younger ministers of the Church of Scotland. These were published in *The Expository Times* between November and March 1940-41 (Vol. LII, numbers 2-6), and one article followed in July (number 10). I wish to thank the editors and Messrs. T. and T. Clark for permission to use this material. It has here been revised and expanded. Another part of the book grew out of lectures given to professors and ministers of the same Church at a conference on ' Theological Education and the World-wide Church ', in July 1941. As one of the organizers of this conference, the Reverend J. W. C. Dougall, says, ' What we need is a bigger view of the Church's task and the kind of world in which a man has to discharge his ministry. That is where the whole picture of the world-wide Church comes in, and any consideration of theological training in which this does not play a big part is just completely out of date.' It is to be hoped that there will be a general re-shaping not only of theological, but of all religious education against the background of that which I take to be the greatest event in modern history—the emergence of the Universal Church, no longer an ideal only, but a fact.

JOHN FOSTER

SELLY OAK COLLEGES,
   BIRMINGHAM.
      September 1, 1941.

[1] Adolf Lowe, *The Universities in Transformation*, 1941, italics mine.

PART I

THE RUIN OF THE WORLD AND
THE UPBUILDING OF THE CHURCH

CHAPTER I

THE FALL OF A CITY

I WAS half-way to church when the sirens sounded. I opened my bag and took out my air-raid-warden's tin hat, saying somewhat ruefully to the preaching gown which reposed below, 'It is not you I shall be wanting after all.'

Which things are a parable. The world in which we used to compose little moral homilies and deliver them as sermons is coming down. Indeed it has already fallen.

Some of us had opportunity to recognize it earlier. A year before our own war started I came home one evening to find my little daughter in tears before the wireless set. The six o'clock news had just come through. She had heard the measured tones of the announcer say, 'To-day Japanese tanks entered the city of Canton.' Most of us heard it, and it meant another dot on a distant war-map. She heard it and it broke her heart. She was born there. It meant her nurse, her playmates, her friends. It is a privilege to begin life with the other side of the world in your heart, but it is a costly privilege when the world is going to pieces. I thought of our Lord weeping over Jerusalem—the fall of a city.

It has come nearer now: Warsaw, Oslo, Rotterdam,

Brussels, Paris—a city? It is the fall of Europe before the barbarian. Still more, a world of ideals has come tumbling down. Someone remarked to me, 'I find our charwoman's morale excellent, but the minister is most depressing. It seems to have got him down.' *Væ victis!* Has the Christian gospel itself come down in the cataclysm?

During the time when I was a China missionary I used to find myself at S.C.M. and other student conferences at intervals of about six years. The intervals made more striking the changes in the idealisms of Christian youth. On one furlough I found that nearly all theologues had gone pacifist. A few collective-security men remained to keep me company, but most had gone the whole way of denying the use of force. How we argued about it! It seemed to threaten the brotherhood of the ministry; it might even bring fresh division to the Church. And how much has either of our rival idealisms really mattered? That was in 1931, the year when Japan invaded Manchuria, and there began the series of betrayals which was to show our collective system to be a hollow mockery. Other aggressions were to follow, ding-dong, east to west and back again, until now . . . down it has all come, like the fall of a city. Pacifists thought in those days that if war came, they would at least have the glory of some mild martyrdom. For the most part the tide of destruction rushes by, and leaves them with the less satisfying rôle of irrelevance.

Next time I came I was struck by the leftward swing. Not so sure of their pacifism, the hearts of young idealists were in Spain. Some were even then ready to fight the Fascist. Communism was the fashion. I was almost shocked. It may have been conservative middle age creeping on. But China is a country where we had seen something more bloody than your theoretic redness. Christian Communists! Some were to feel later that they had to swallow those words. And it was hard to get them down after the sickening events of the winter of 1939-40. More of our ideals had turned out to be mere idealizations, and withered among the ruins of East Poland and in the snows of the Mannerheim Line.

A better world, a juster society—what are we left with? Has our religion to crawl back into mere individualism, and take its place along with that other refuge, the Anderson shelter, in our own back garden?

There are those who say so, and bring an impressive theology to prove it. In one group at the World Christian Conference at Madras in 1938,[1] we were discussing the function of the missionary. Someone suggested that we ought not to omit mention of his services as peace-maker, strengthening the foundations of international understanding. A continental delegate protested: ' The foundations of peace cannot be laid. The life of the State cannot be made Christian. " The whole world lieth in the evil one." Everything must get worse and worse . . . until peace comes from above.'

Someone passed round that ribald parody,

> ' Sit down, O men of God,
>   His kingdom He will bring
> Whenever He desireth it—
>   You cannot do a thing.'

[1] The meeting of the International Missionary Council at Tambaram, Madras, December 12-29, 1938.

Perhaps by this time we have no laughter left for anyone's despair.

Are we to submit to this religious pessimism which, even before the Nazi invasion, had captured the Protestants of the Continent? Are we to regard Christianity as that which prepares our hearts to greet His coming on the clouds of heaven?

The Christian life lived in separation from the world, rather than in influence upon it, with a hope which is altogether other-worldly, and as complete a handing over of this world-order to the devil, these are not upstart ideas without a history. There is a sermon which some day I should like to preach on: ' The Fall of a City '. Start from Rabshakeh in the Second Book of Kings, chapter xviii, the challenge of the pagan aggressor: ' Who are they among the gods . . . that have delivered their country out of my hand, that the Lord should deliver Jerusalem? ' Then Psalm cxxxvii:

> ' How shall we sing the Lord's song
> In a strange land?
> If I forget thee, O Jerusalem,
> Let my right hand forget her cunning,
> Let my tongue cleave to the roof of my mouth,
> If I remember thee not.'

The worst has happened: the Lord has not delivered Jerusalem. Then that other Man, who weeps for the city: ' O Jerusalem, Jerusalem . . . Behold, your house is left unto you desolate ' (Luke xiii. 34f.). And then when again the worst has happened, when the armies of Titus have breached the walls, desecrated and destroyed the temple, and left only a huddle of ruins: ' I saw the holy city, new Jerusalem, coming down out of heaven from God. . . . And the nations shall walk amidst the light thereof, and the kings of the earth do bring their glory into it ' (Revelation xxi). There, for first-century Christians, when the light had been put out shone a transcendent faith which enabled them to go on.

What did it mean? There were from the beginning those who said that it meant separatist other-worldliness. But that, as we are coming clearly to see, does not take the full measure of Christian Apocalypse. Certainly it does not represent the main stream of the Church's life. Other-worldly Christianity is not the mark of the Catholics, but of the sects—Montanists in the second century and Donatists in the fourth. It finds what is to remain for a thousand years its most typical expression in the beginnings of monasticism. Every monastic revival is in some measure a renewed forsaking of the world. When we leave the Middle Ages, we find that this is the emphasis of continental Protestantism. Our ancestors brought something of it home, first from Wittenberg, then from Zurich, Strasbourg, Frankfort, and Geneva.

We whose spiritual ancestry has come by way of these movements have long ago departed from the tradition of our fathers. The Kingdom of God for which we have worked and prayed was one which was being worked out in the here and now. It ought to have meant our coming to a less one-sided apprehension, that is, a more *catholic* apprehension, of the Christian faith. Often it has meant that we have let go other-worldliness, and grasped nothing more substantial than . . . (shall we say?) a diffused ' social gospel ' as that which was to be proclaimed, a vague

Christian internationalism as Christianity's fulfilment in this world. No wonder our idealisms have come tumbling down.

I am always trying to persuade people, as a Church History teacher should, that you cannot appreciate Christianity, nor even understand our Lord, with the Bible alone. You need the Church. So now let us follow that theme, the fall of a city, into one period of Church History.

If you want an example of a naïve ending to a learned book read the *De Civitate Dei* of St. Augustine. It is rather a long way to read just for the ending; the English translation amounts to about half a million words. This is how it ends:

> ' Let those who think that I have said too little,
> and those who think that I have said too much,
>   forgive me,
> and let those who think that I have said just
>   enough,
> give thanks to God with me.—Amen.'

Well, Augustine, dear Father-in-God, I am one who thinks that you have said too much. Yet I not only forgive you, but give thanks. For of all the Fathers of the Church, none has more to offer to our present need.

The previous breakdown of Western civilization was at a time when the Church in the West was still young —the fall of Rome before Alaric the Visigoth in the year 410. The light of civilization was put out. The six hundred years which we call the Dark Ages began.

The news filled all men with foreboding and profound dismay. Jerome, the scholar-monk, heard it in his cell at Bethlehem. He was a monk and had left the world, so might have been superior to the world's sorrows. But he was a scholar, and the triumph of barbarism was like a sword piercing his soul.

' My tongue,' he writes, ' cleaves to the roof of my mouth and my voice is choked with sobs, to think that that city is captive which led captive the whole world.'[1]

It is heartening to see how differently Augustine faced it. When the hearts of most men were sick with fear, this elderly bishop—he was approaching sixty— began to write a book. The book took him almost all the rest of his life to finish.[2] And it was called, not as an old man's book at such a time might well have been, Memoirs of the City of Rome, but Concerning the City of God. Let him describe its origin himself:

' After the storming and the sack of Rome by the Goths . . . my zeal was kindled for the house of God, and I was induced to defend the City of God against the calumnies and misrepresentations of its foes.'[3]

So from one of the world's most grievous calamities was born the Church's grandest apology. In some ways it is the most imposing and epoch-making apology of all time.[4]

It is impossible adequately to summarize this im-

---

[1] Epistles, cxxvii. In justice to Jerome, compare Epistles, lx, ' The Roman world is falling, yet we hold up our heads instead of bowing them down.'

[2] It seems to have been written between the years 413 and 426.

[3] Retractions, xliii.

[4] See Monument to St. Augustine, especially in the contribution by Mr. Christopher Dawson, pp. 72-77.

mense work in the space at our disposal. I want to
draw attention to its relevance in two respects: Augustine says we must not let go our other-worldliness,
nor must we be content with vague Christian
idealisms.

Augustine begins by answering that inevitable
question of times of calamity, ' Where is thy God? '[1]
Some are saying that disaster has overtaken Rome
because the Empire has forsaken its old gods for the
God of the Christians. No, says Augustine. The fact
is that the old gods could not have saved Rome. But
Christianity, if it has not saved the city, has tempered
the calamity in ways never seen before. The barbarians have respected the sanctuary of Christian
churches, and spared the lives of all, Christian and
pagan, who fled for refuge there.[2]

Does not that remind you of those vast refugee
camps on mission compound and college campus
during China's years of war? Some of the parallels
are extraordinarily close:

' In a Chinese town captured not long ago a woman
was in the hands of a Japanese soldier. To her amazement she found herself taken to the door of a little chapel
and handed over to the Chinese pastor, with the words,
" This woman is in great danger. I give her into your
Christian hands. I too am a Christian." '[3]

Rarer in and around Nanking, it is the same scene
of which Augustine had been told by those who
escaped from the sack of Rome: The horrors of war,
he says, were not new, but

[1] Psalm xlii. 3, 10, etc., quoted in Book I, 29.
[2] Book I, 1, 2.
[3] *Lift up your Heads*, United Society for Christian Literature,
report for the year 1939-40, p. 7.

'. . . what was new was that savage barbarians showed themselves in so gentle a guise that the largest churches were chosen and set apart for the purpose of being filled with the people to whom quarter was given. . . . Into them were led by their relenting enemies many to be set free, and from them none was led to slavery by merciless foes.'[1]

In Rome also the reason is that there are those among the invaders—in numbers far more—who would say, 'I too am a Christian.'

'Whoever does not see that this is to be attributed to the name of Christ is blind; whoever sees and gives no praise, is ungrateful; whoever hinders another from praising is mad.'[2]

We must acknowledge as an exception what Augustine claims as the rule. But the numbers saved by the great organized refugee camps in China must be larger by many times than those for whom the basilicas of Rome could provide a sanctuary.

In these cases the invader has withheld slaughter and rape, not indeed out of respect for the Christians' God, but because of British and American nationals in the missionary body. To Chinese it has been an immense object lesson—'see how these Christians love'. Christianity has tempered the calamity as nothing else could.[3]

It is true of the whole calamity of this war-torn world. The progress of scientific civilization may be neutral: we invent the petrol engine and then use it alike for the bombing plane, and the motor ambulance,

[1] Book I, 7. [2] Book I, 7.
[3] Well described, e.g. in *Christians in Action* (Longmans, 1938).

which bears away the victims.   It may be wholly evil:
it gives us the bomb, poison gas, the tank, the Bren
gun.   But how dreadful if among it all had not
stood Christian men claiming some of our advancing
knowledge for works of mercy—the anæsthetic, the
surgeon's skill, the nurse's menial service sancti-
fied, Christian 'big business' which organizes relief,
Christians blessed with this world's goods who
support the same.   Christianity does temper the
calamity.

But the major part of these first five books is
not given to this argument.   Augustine goes on
to acknowledge that 'God and evil suffer alike
in this world.   But though the sufferings are the
same, the sufferers are not. . . . The difference lies
not in the suffering, but in the way in which it is
borne.'[1]

That is the first point: *Augustine recalls us to a
proper other-worldliness.*

'They lost all they had. . . . But did they lose their
faith? Did they lose their godliness? Did they lose the
treasures of the heart? This is the wealth of the
Christian.'[2]

He chooses as an example one wealthy Christian
who, in poverty after the barbarians had looted his
home, was able to say: 'Lord, let me not be troubled
for gold and silver, for where all my treasure is Thou
knowest.'[3]

'It is not of importance whether life be long or short
. . . but it is of importance how a man dies. . . . That
death is not to be accounted a calamity which was preceded by a good life.'[4]

[1] Book I, 8.   [2] Book I, 10.   [3] Book I, 10.   [4] Book I, 11.

' The whole family of God most high and true has a consolation of its own, one that does not fail. . . . In this mortal life a man is trained for life eternal.'[1]

We will not follow the argument as it is developed and illustrated through the rest of this part of the work. The importance for us here is that Augustine recalls us to a proper other-worldliness.

The second part, Books VI to X, is a defence against those who say that this other-worldly hope could be adequately provided by the old religions. It is splendid apologetic, presented with a wealth of inside knowledge. Augustine himself had come to the Christian faith by way of Neo-platonism, that fairest flowering of pre-Christian philosophy. It always strikes me with amazement that he did not feel that the urgency of the times meant concentration on merely practical Christianity to the neglect of dogmatic. Here you will go with Augustine deep down to the theological bases of the faith— while the Empire, while civilized life, is falling in ruins!

Then come twelve Books (XI-XXII) which really take up the main theme, the Two Cities. It is here that Augustine makes, from the point of view of our present need, his second great contribution. He does not leave us with mere other-worldliness. Let us begin with his own summary: ' The human race we have divided into two parts, those who live according to man, and those who live according to God, and these we mystically call the Two Cities.'[2] He traces this twofold division from the beginning of history:

[1] Book I, 29.   [2] Book XV, 1.

Adam has two sons. Cain ' builded a city and called
the name of the city . . . Enoch.'[1] Abel is a shepherd with no fixed habitation, prototype of Christ the
Shepherd of our souls.[2] It was the builder of the
earthly city who slew the shepherd. Then comes the
building of the tower of Babel, which he identifies
with the city of Babylon. ' And the Lord came down
to see the city and the tower which the sons of men
built,'[3] and because they vied with heaven He brought
their work to nought. Third, is Abraham,[4] who left
a city with Lot. But Lot chose the city of Sodom,
while Abraham waited for the fulfilment of larger
promises. And so to Moses[5] and the separation of
God's people from Egypt. In the period of the Kings
there is the distinction between Saul and David; the
kingdom and the priesthood; the division of the kingdom itself; all of them signs of that perpetual division
of temporal and spiritual which is to be made complete in Christ. In Book XVIII he turns back to point
out the relation of all this to secular history: Assyria,
Argos, Egypt, Athens, Troy, Latium, Rome, Persia,
these with their mixtures of history and legend are
the setting of the sacred story which gives them all
significance.

Much of it may try your patience and seem altogether too fanciful to contain anything of permanent
worth. But the point is that it is the first attempt at
a Christian philosophy of history. Augustine is seeing
all history with the purpose of God, *and the people of*

---

[1] Genesis iv. 17.
[2] Augustine's fancy is really more involved: Abel=' grief ', and
Seth=' resurrection '. Faith in these, the passion and resurrection
of our Lord, is set over against reliance on this world, Book XV, 18.
[3] Book XVI, 4. [4] Book XVI, 12 onwards. [5] Book XVI, 43.

God, central in it. And this while the world is going to pieces!

This is the implication of what he is saying: For three generations now people have been used to thinking of the Church as the State Church of the Roman Empire. But it is not. The Roman Empire is ' the earthly city which shall not be everlasting '. The Church is composed of ' sojourners in that earthly city whose citizenship is in the heavenly Jerusalem '. The Empire had existed in the purposes of God only for the sake of the Church. The Church has used the *pax Romana,* the Greek language, the Roman roads, the safety of the sea-routes. Now, if it has served its turn . . . Augustine is able to stand at the end of an age and look into the darkness. He is looking ahead to six hundred years of barbarism, to the slow emergence of a rough feudal society, as the new environment for the Church. For empires may rise and fall, world orders change, civilizations vanish, but ' the City of God remaineth '.

Can we face it? We look into the darkness of a new age. We believe that the tide of barbarism will be stemmed and swept back. But even so, it will leave a Europe in ruins, an Empire impoverished; the centre of commerce in London and of culture in Paris may never fully return from across the Atlantic. We do not know. But what we ought to know is that we belong first, not to Europe, not to the Empire, but to the City of God. We need to return, from the diffused Christian idealisms which before we sought first as His kingdom and His righteousness, to a higher churchmanship. Christians must become again men who know what it is which claims and holds their ultimate loyalties, what it is for which they live, for sake of which they would be content to die, ' the Church which is His body, the fulness of Him that filleth all in all.'[1]

[1] Ephesians i. 22f.

CHAPTER II

THE CITY OF GOD REMAINETH

THE connexion between Augustine, Bishop of Hippo, and Augustine, Archbishop of Canterbury, may seem to be only casual. It is really causal. If, with the world falling in ruins about him, the first had not written his *De Civitate Dei* I doubt if our heathen ancestors would ever have seen the second. The Anglo-Saxons were among the most savage of those barbarians who fifteen hundred years ago invaded the Roman Empire and put out the light of Western civilization. A century and a half later (597) missionaries of the Roman Church were invading Kent, and rekindling the light of the Christian gospel. The second Augustine came because the first had believed, taught, and stamped it upon the minds of his successors that the kingdoms of this world may change but the City of God goes on a-building.

His faith was justified—or rather it so happened because he passed on such faith. The Church had at first been disliked and despised by the Empire, ' a class hated for their abominations, called Christians by the vulgar '.[1] Later it had been adopted and used by the Empire, ' to set in order the body of the world, labouring under grievous sickness '.[2] Now it had outlasted

[1] Tacitus, *Annales*, XV, 44.
[2] One of the descriptions by Constantine of the use he hoped to make of the Church.

the Empire. Soon it was to reclaim lands lost to the
Empire—lands towards which there was no more in
the West any imperial power to stretch out its hands.
The Church was to become more central in the life
of the new Europe than it could ever have been in that
of the old Empire.

This last stage, subject of Augustine's prophetic
vision, is often described with a different emphasis.
The prophet who writes before the event understands
better than the historian who comes after:

> ' In the rise of the Papacy on the spot left desolate by
> the Empire the mysterious power of the old city claimed
> the future as her own by breathing her stern spirit of
> aggression into the power of love and brotherhood which
> had begun to bind the world into a vaster system than
> even the Roman Empire had created.'[1]

This is a noble sentence, rightly acknowledging the
magnitude of the Church's missionary achievement,
begun under such bishops of Rome as Gregory the
Great. It is spoiled by that reference to the old city.
' The mysterious power ' was the power of the City
of God. Before the fall of Rome in 410, there had
already been evident a transference of loyalty from
the city as the capital of an earthly empire, to the city
as the focal point on earth of the eternal Kingdom :

> ' It is for this that I admire the city (of Rome), not
> for its much gold, for its columns, nor for any other
> phantasy, but because of these two Pillars of the Church
> (SS. Peter and Paul). Who will grant me to embrace the
> body of Paul, to cling to his sepulchre, to see the dust of
> that body which " filled up that which was lacking " in

[1] Creighton, *History of the Papacy*, p. 6.

Christ, which bore His stigmata, and sowed His teaching everywhere? '[1]

After 410 what mysterious power remained about the city of Rome but that of Holy Church? It was the sense of that power, and of its continuing though the world lay in ruins, which Augustine handed on.

He did indeed hand it on. He had already been busy some five years with his *De Civitate Dei* when Leo, a youthful acolyte from Rome, employed as letter-bearer between Italian and North African bishops,[2] came into touch with him. In the year 440 Leo became Pope. 'The first Pope' some have called him. 'The Great' all men acknowledge. It is with him that the change takes place: the sceptre which falls from the hands of the Emperor is firmly grasped by the Bishop of Rome. Politically, the desolation and decay which Augustine has witnessed are but one generation more advanced. The Huns (451) and the Vandals (455) follow to ravage where the Goths have led the way. But Leo does not need to write an apology for the fall of the city. It is he who saves the city from falling. He can speak, not merely as prophet of a new day, but as guardian of the faith in a day which has already opened. Like Chrysostom he extols (in a sermon for June 29th, the day of their festival) the Apostles Peter and Paul, but with still greater confidence:[3]

'These are they who promoted thee (the city of Rome) to such glory, that being made a holy nation, a chosen

---

[1] Chrysostom, *Homilies on the Epistles to the Romans*, xxxii. St. John Chrysostom died three years before the fall of Rome.
[2] Augustine, *Epistles*, cxci, cxciv.   [3] *Sermons*, lxxxii.

people, a priestly and royal state, and the head of the world through the blessed Peter's holy See, thou didst attain a wider sway by the worship of God than by earthly government. Although thou wert increased by many victories, and didst extend thy rule on land and sea, yet that which thy toils in war subdued is less than that which the peace of Christ has conquered.'

The quotation from Chrysostom conveniently raises a question—perhaps mention of Leo and of the Papacy hastens it—a question which in any case could not long be kept back. At the end of the previous chapter, I too quoted a passage about filling up that which was lacking, that daring description of the Church in Ephesians i. 22f. Our accustomed English is a mistranslation dating back to Tyndale. It should read:

' The Church which is His body, the fulfilment of Him who is being out-and-out fulfilled.'[1]

I quoted this passage to express the superlative worth of that which, beyond nation and culture and empire, and beyond all lesser idealisms, still claims our ultimate allegiance. It will inevitably be asked, Is not that to over-emphasize the Church as a visible institution?

Our Protestant way has been to accept such lofty expositions as applying to the Church triumphant. Our forefathers were compelled to challenge the authority of the ecclesiastical hierarchy, and their sons have never recovered from it. Some have even grown accustomed to speaking lightly of the Church

[1] Cf. J. Armitage Robinson, *St. Paul's Epistle to the Ephesians*, pp. 42-45, 152.

militant, as ' organized religion '. Surely the whole meaning of the Church as His body is that it is in some sense His second incarnation. He has no hands to do His will, no feet to walk His way, no voice to call men, apart from the *ecclesia*. The Church, doing these services for Him, does them imperfectly: anon there is a Judas who betrays, a Peter who denies, others who forsake Him and flee. Such is still the price of His humiliation. The Church is becoming, not has become. But its completion as the instrument of His purposes, or rather His fulfilment in the Church, is not left in doubt. Christ is being ' out-and-out fulfilled '. For the sake of Him whose body it shall perfectly become, we serve that which is becoming.

To those who believe distantly in the Church as the totality of the elect, and meanwhile consider their more immediate duty the spread of His Kingdom in the world—the leaven of Christian ideals, a more Christian social order, peace, and a Christian atmosphere for international relations—I would say two things: First, a transcendent Church ideal has no meaning unless it is related to that which persists among us. Second, we mistake our heritage—a disembodied Christianity never would have persisted. These causes which we serve and call His Kingdom would not be there at all but for the central fact of the Church, even the Church on earth with all its shortcomings. At this time when so many of our more diffused idealisms have come to disillusion, we are recalled to the central fact. We need to know that it is the Church for which we must live; that the Church has that whereby the world itself must live; and that in a ruined world the City of God remaineth.

Such is the faith of Augustine:

'This heavenly City then, while it sojourns on earth, calls citizens out of all nations, and gathers together a society of pilgrims of all languages, not scrupling about diversities in their manners, laws, institutions. . . . It even preserves and adopts these diversities so long as no hindrance to the worship of the one supreme God is thereby introduced. This alone can be truly called . . . peace . . . the perfectly ordered and harmonious enjoyment of God, and enjoyment of one another in God. In its pilgrim state the heavenly City possesses this peace by faith; and by this faith it lives righteously . . . for the life of the City is a social life.'[1]

There is a surprisingly Augustinian strain in the call which was sounded from the Madras Conference. I will quote one paragraph where you will find in other words the same three points made by Augustine above: (1) The Church is a world-wide Church; (2) the Church has the secret of true peace; (3) the life of the Church is the actualization of the Christian's faith for society:

'In all humility and penitence we are constrained to declare to a baffled and needy world that the Christian Church, under God, is its greatest hope. The decade since last we met has witnessed the progressive rending of the fabric of humanity; it has witnessed an increasing unification of the body of Christ. As we meet here from over sixty nations out of every continent we have discovered afresh that that unity is not merely an inspiration but a fact. . . . Our nations are at war with one another; but we know ourselves brethren in the community of Christ's Church. Our peoples increase in suspicion and

---

[1] *De Civitate Dei*, Book XIX, 17.

fear of one another; but we are learning to trust each other more deeply through common devotion to the one Lord of us all. Our governments build instruments of mutual destruction; we join in united action for the reconciliation of humanity. Thus in broken and imperfect fashion the Church is even now fulfilling its calling to be within itself a foretaste of the redeemed family of God which He has purposed humanity to be. . . . By faith, but in deep assurance, we declare that this body which God has fashioned through Christ cannot be destroyed.'[1]

The City of God remaineth! Is it true? We saw that Augustine's faith was rewarded. What right have we to expect that ours will be? Let us look at it point by point.

(1) *The Church is a world-wide Church.* Just before going to that World Conference at Madras, I met an ex-India missionary in a London street. He knew me as ex-China, and said, 'We'll show you something of real missionary work now! We've got the biggest thing in the world, the outcaste movement.' In no business is it wise to let a competitor crack up his wares and get away with it. So I said, ' The biggest thing in the world? Perhaps you mean the most spectacular.' He leaned nearer to me and said, ' It is the answer to much that is happening on this side of the world.' And he was gone. For a moment I forgot the London street; I forgot the city of London; and I remembered the City of God. Now that I have seen with my own eyes, I shall never forget.

[1] *The World Mission of the Church*, p. 19; *The Authority of the Faith*. Tambaram Madras Series, Vol. I, pp. 192f. It needs no expert literary critic to recognize the composite nature of this document. Another strain keeps recurring which seems suspicious of this emphasis on the Church, and seeks to modify it with that which I have called diffused idealism concerning the Kingdom.

Something is happening on a scale which it is hard to parallel. 'A great door and effectual is opened.'[1] No, that is no longer the picture. The Church has had to put a foot against the door lest it should be stampeded. Even so, outcastes are coming in at the rate of three thousand a week, and there are seventy millions of them:

'If it has mattered to the whole world that seventy million people in Russia twenty years ago set their faces towards Marxism, how much will it matter if about the same number in India now ask us to show them the Christian way of life?'[2]

What one received on going to Madras was not only, nor mainly, some knowledge of Indian situations, but glimpses of the world Church over against world need. I have been trying to frame statements about other parts of the world which might stand with that just quoted. Here are two of my attempts, which I submit are just as startling, and just as true:

If it matters to the world that some two hundred and fifty millions in Europe live under the domination of the Nazi clique, who persecute religion and encourage paganism to rear again its ugly head, how much will it matter that four hundred and fifty millions in China should be finding unity to meet their crisis in the leadership of a Christian and should remain loyal to his government though temporarily invaded?

If we almost lose hope when we see the dark ages outclassed in the widespread savagery of anti-Jewish pogroms, what hope do we take when we remember that of the only race which has been still more vilely wronged, the Negro, seven per cent. have now been claimed as brothers in Christ?[3]

[1] 1 Corinthians xvi. 9.
[2] G. E. Phillips, *The Untouchables' Quest*, p. 9.
[3] *Interpretative Statistical Survey of the World Mission*, p. 240.

So one might go on. Link your lonely disillusioned individual strivings to the great task of the world Church, and you will see already in fact what Augustine could see only with the eye of faith, the Church as the centre of a new Christendom which is being built up to help to redress the balance of the old. The City of God remaineth.

(2) *The Church has the secret of true peace.* The above section may seem to advocate a mere geographic transfer of attention, from lands of despair to areas of hope. What we need is more than that; it is (to borrow a phrase used as a title for the popular account of the Madras Conference) ' through Tragedy to Triumph,'[1] a faith which, like Augustine's, not only sees over the ruins but rises in their very midst. We need seek no further than Lord Halifax's words when he was Foreign Minister:

' To ignore the obligations of fellowship with those younger churches . . . would be at once failure and betrayal. For it would mean loss of hope and inspiration won through a common life in which peoples of all races may be united. We should surely be playing truant from a school where we can best learn many of the secrets essential to the building of the better world of our desires.'[2]

Reading those words one hears the voice, not of the statesman of a nation engaged in total war, but of a son of the Church and a servant of the City of God.

' Peoples of all races may be united . . .' I was privileged to see the following letter from a missionary in North China, where the tide of war has swept

[1] By Basil Mathews.
[2] Letter to *The Times*, November 26, 1939.

over, and (so it seemed at first), almost engulfed the Church:

'I cannot close this letter without a tribute to the attitude of Chinese Christians towards the people of Japan, especially towards Christians there. They pray for them as they do for the Church in China, and really feel that their union in Christ is stronger than all that separates. This is especially noticeable when a Japanese Christian soldier comes to church. We are living in the midst of an armed camp and from time to time do have such a visitor. The expression of strain and apprehension on seeing him vanishes as he says, "I also am a Christian." Last Sunday one came, in his own country a teacher of a Sunday-school class, now conscripted as a private in the transportation corps. One of our young teachers when she heard who and what he was, said, "What a pity! What a waste!" The Japanese soldier had a talk with the Chinese minister. On leaving, since he was about to go to the front he asked for a verse from the Chinese Bible, with the minister's signature, to carry in his cap. The verse the Chinese minister gave him was, "Where there cannot be Greek and Jew, . . . barbarian, Scythian, bondman, freeman: but Christ is all, and in all." '[1]

As I folded the letter, I said, 'The City of God remaineth.'

'. . . The building of the better world of our desires.' One Englishman, with no previous experience of Chinese people, on returning from the Madras Conference said that the most impressive of all the national delegations was the forty or so members from China. 'Here in the West,' he explained, 'people are saying that the next war, if it comes, will be the end. In China it has come. But these Chinese Chris-

---

[1] Colossians iii. 11.

tian leaders do not speak of it as the end. They regard the ruin of their national life as their opportunity to rebuild it more nearly according to the mind of Christ.' That is not typical Chinese courage. There is no such thing. Courage has never been much of a virtue—in China no one is ashamed of saying that he is afraid. It is Christian courage, and it is true to type: ' This is the victory that overcometh the world, even our faith.'[1]

(3) *The life of the Church is the actualization of the Christian faith for society.* By roundabout ways the first news, since the Nazi invasion of the Low Countries, was months later received of a distinguished European delegate to Madras. In the letter comes this cryptic sentence which no Nazi censor would understand: ' How splendid that God gave us December 1938[2] before May 1940.'

There is a widespread tendency to indulge in self-pity. Twice in one lifetime we have seen the breakdown of Western civilization in ghastly war. Was ever a generation like ours? This attitude is, again, the result of fixing our attention on ' civilization ', on Christendom, on the vaguer idealisms which gather round the Church, and the diffused influences which radiate from it, instead of knowing that that which matters supremely is the central fact, the life of the Church itself. We see May 1940; many of us have never heard of December 1938.

As we gathered at Madras, representatives of Christ's Church from almost every land under the

[1] 1 John v. 4.
[2] The date of the Madras meeting.

sun,[1] some of us thought we heard our Lord saying,
'Blessed are the eyes which see the things that ye
see: for I say unto you, that many prophets and
kings desired to see the things which ye see, and
saw them not.'[2]   Yes, indeed, was ever a generation
like ours?   The universal nature of the Church, true
as an ideal from the time of our Lord and His
Apostles, we saw as no Christians in nineteen centuries
have seen, worthily represented in the actual and the
concrete.   This also has happened in our lifetime.
God is not mocked.   The world is not left at the
mercy of a madman.   Present in God's world, and
never so widely established, is God's Church, the
central point of His working, the instrument for the
fulfilment of His purposes, already in itself ' a foretaste of the redeemed family of God which He has
purposed humanity to be '.   The City of God remaineth.   Lift up your hearts!

[1] For list of members, see *Addresses and Other Records,* Tambaram Madras Series, Vol. VII, 181-202.
[2] Luke x. 23f.

CHAPTER III

THE CHURCHES AND THE CHURCH

I HAVE tried to keep our feet upon the earth. But someone says, ' It is easy to talk about the Church. All that we know is the churches.' This must give us pause. It is something not to be overlooked by anyone discussing present need.

I was not assigned to the group which at Madras worked on Co-operation and Unity.[1] One day I met one of its most responsible members rubbing his hands with glee. ' The delegates of the Younger Churches,' he said, ' when they frame a resolution, do not dress it up or tone it down as we do. Listen to this:

' " The divisions of Christendom are seen in their worst light on the mission field . . . disgraceful competition . . . wasteful overlapping . . . a stumbling-block to the faithful . . . a mockery to those without . . . bringing dishonour to the religion of our Master . . . the scandalous effects of our divisions." '

Perhaps it was the difference between intemperate youth and circumspect middle-age. But anyone who wrote of our divisions from the midst of the Madras

[1] *The Life of the Church*, Tambaram Madras Series, Vol. IV, pp. 397-404, especially 402.

Conference of 1938 would have written strongly. For a blessed period of three weeks it was as though they did not exist. We knew, as not one of us had known before, what it meant to belong to the Universal Church. Am I exaggerating if I say that we knew it as no one in nineteen centuries of the Church's history had had a chance to know?

The crowded events of the months since make these experiences seem distant. But they are some of the things which I nowadays most often feel called to preach about. It is no small consolation, while European Christendom is being battered into ruins, to give to God's people the assurance that the day of the Universal Church has come, that His Church was never so widespread, His redeemed family, the central point of His working for the achievement of His purposes for the world.

Those are high-sounding words. Are they anything more? I have sometimes doubted when my sermon was over, hymn sung, blessing given, and I was standing at the church door. We belong to the Universal Church, but consider its local manifestation! There is a rival show across the way. The spire of another rises just down the street. Everything is a reminder of that which is partial, divided, ineffectual. Instead of meeting the challenge of our day as becomes the army of the Lord, we are reduced to scattered squads of skirmishers, who are incapable of any sustained offensive and cannot even hold the line. In one respect I disagree with the resolution of those delegates of the Younger Churches, ' The divisions of Christendom are seen in their worst light on the mission field.' As I look round here at home I doubt if that is true any longer. Still, let us start with the Younger Churches.

'A mockery to those without': Dr. Hu Shih, leader of China's modern Renaissance, is a man who believes that his country had better risk losing some features of her old culture rather than fail to grasp with both hands the blessings of Western science and the standard of life made possible by our machine-civilization.[1] This attitude prevails among Chinese nationalists—in marked contrast to that of the *khaddar*-clad[2] followers of Mr. Gandhi, who urge India's return to the spinning-wheel as part of the national salvation. One might have expected this openness to all that is best from abroad to imply an open ear to the message of the Church. But this is a sample of what Dr. Hu Shih has to say about religion:

'It is well for you to say that Christianity is better than our Taoism and Buddhism.'

(I think he is ready to agree so far—it would be entirely in accordance with his principles for him to do so.)

'But in Christianity there are one or two hundred different denominations attacking each other. Which denomination shall we adopt?'

He exaggerates—it is not two hundred. But in China there are 132 missionary societies, which seems a sufficient advertisement of our shame.

[1] *China Christian Year Book*, 1929, p. 115.
[2] Cloth produced on the hand-loom.

The work of the most important of these has resulted in the growth of major churches to the number of twelve, the largest being that federal-union of churches which is called the Church of Christ in China. This is largely of Presbyterian and Congregationalist origin. It comprises nearly one quarter of the whole of non-Roman Christians. These twelve major churches make up 86 per cent. of the total. The remaining 14 per cent., the work of some forty missionary societies, may be described as the ' small fancies ' of left-wing Protestantism, some of them in their exclusive intolerance being a match for the Church of Rome itself.

It is bad enough. And I was told of worse in India. I never fail to feel the sting of shame in that story of the low-caste tribe which had all but made up its mind to come over to the Christian Church. Then a clever Hindu lawyer pointed out that as a community they were scattered over a wide territory. In different parts of it different societies were at work. Hinduism stands for caste unity; Christianity is that which divides. The lawyer won his point, and the mass-movement did not happen. In discussing India's political future we often point to her religions as a divisive force: communal strife between Hindu and Moslem; within Hinduism the separation of high caste from low; the exclusion of the ' untouchables '. Did we realize that the Hindu can point the finger of scorn to our religion as threatening even such unity as exists? ' A mockery to those without ': so it is.

Some, so far from agreeing that our divisions mean failure, believe that diversity, being a sign of vitality, is an earnest of success. There is something in this.

The typical expression of revival in the medieval Church was a new monastic order. It is in an entirely similar way that in the parts of the Western Church which broke with the Roman hierarchy a burst of new life takes shape in a new community—a denomination. The tragedy is that, whereas in the Middle Ages the Church was generally ready to expand its boundaries and reconsider its rules in order to make room for these disturbances in its routine life, too often in Protestant communions a spring of new life has been unrecognized, or unwelcomed by those who stood for a traditional church order, and the resulting new community has been thrust outside. This is especially so in England. Through a proper concern for preserving the national unity in the dangers of Elizabeth's reign, our country developed a habit—and the habit continued right down to the Anglican Revival in the middle of last century: leaders of movements of distinctive religious vitality were told to get down, and, when they refused, to get out. They ought to have been taken up and assimilated into the life of an undivided English Church.

Macaulay was writing history as well as wit when he said:

'Far different is the policy of Rome. The ignorant enthusiast whom the Anglican Church makes an enemy, and whatever the polite and learned may think, a most dangerous enemy, the Catholic Church makes a champion. She bids him nurse his beard, covers him with a gown and hood of coarse dark stuff, ties a rope round his waist, and sends him forth to teach in her name. He costs her nothing. He takes not a ducat away from the revenues of her beneficed clergy. He lives by the alms of those who respect his spiritual character, and are grateful for his instructions. . . . In this way the Church of Rome unites in herself all the strength of establishment and all the strength of dissent. With the utmost pomp of a dominant hierarchy above, she has all the energy of the voluntary system below. It would be easy to mention very recent instances in which the hearts of hundreds of thousands, estranged from her by the selfishness, sloth, and cowardice of the beneficed clergy, have been brought back by the zeal of the begging friars.

' Even for female agency there is a place. . . . At Rome the Countess of Huntingdon would have a place in the calendar as Saint Selina, and Mrs. Fry would be foundress and first Superior of the Blessed Order of Sisters of the Gaols.

' Place Ignatius Loyola at Oxford. He is certain to become the head of a formidable secession. Place John Wesley at Rome. He is certain to be the first General of a new society devoted to the interests and honour of the Church.'[1]

I am willing to agree that often diversity is the sign of an abounding vitality, of manifold revival, of movements of the Spirit in unexpected places and people. But when such diversity results in division, something has gone wrong. It may be something in the revival movement. It may be something in the unrevived and unresponsive body of the Church. Diversity is often due to the blessing of God; division is always due to man's mishandling of it.

What division has meant historically to the Church standing over against the non-Christian world is best seen by turning to two events which Professor Latourette labels ' the first and second great losses of territory '.[2] The first is the rise of Islam in the seventh

---

[1] *Essay on Von Ranke's History of the Popes,* 1840.
[2] *A History of the Expansion of Christianity,* II, 286ff., 308ff.

century. The second is the conversion to Islam of the Mongol rulers of Asia about the year 1300.

When, with the German invasions of the fifth century, crisis came to the lands of the Western Church, that Church, under the rising power of the Bishop of Rome, was drawn together into a unity strong enough not only to withstand the shocks of change but to re-expand among the new peoples of Europe. Two centuries later the Church at the eastern end of the Mediterranean had to face the swift outpouring of the Arab power of Islam. Its condition was vastly different: the church of the East (Nestorian), with its Catholicos at the Persian capital and its missionaries already reaching out towards China,[1] had severed its connexion with the Church of the Roman Empire. The West Syrian (Jacobite), Armenian, Coptic and Abyssinian Churches were disaffected; these were all Monophysite, but greater than any Christological difference is their impatience of anything wider than their local loyalties. As a result, the land of our Lord's earthly life, scenes of the labours of His Apostles, the homes of some of the greatest of the Fathers, were overrun by the invader. They became Moslem lands with a small Christian remnant, lands which to this day claim some of the most sacrificial and apparently unrewarded of missionary service. Nearly two hundred and fifty years ago the Dean of Norwich[2] used this illustration, the triumph of Islam in the Near East, as a warning to Christians in England against their divisions:

[1] My *Church of the T'ang Dynasty*, pp. 32ff.
[2] Humphrey Prideaux, *Life of Mahomet* (1697), a polemical tract against the Deists.

' A sad memento to us: for of all Christian Churches now remaining in the world, which is it that hath more reason than we at this present, to learn instruction from this example, and to take warning therefrom? '

In the year 1271 Pope Gregory X received a request immediately upon his ascending the throne of St. Peter. It came from the ruler of the greatest empire the world has ever seen—Kublai Khan. The rule of the Mongols extended from the Ural Mountains to the Himalayas, and from the China Sea to the River Danube.[1] The Great Khan sent Nicolo and Maffeo Polo, Marco's father and uncle, as his ambassadors to the Pope, saying:

' You shall go to your High Priest and shall pray him on our behalf to send me a hundred men skilled in your religion . . . and so I shall be baptized, and when I shall be baptized all my barons and great men will be baptized, and then their subjects will receive baptism, and so there will be more Christians here than there are in your parts.'[2]

Taken along with other evidence of the times—the number of Nestorians in high official position, baptisms even in the Imperial family, the presence of the Church of the East, often a minority, but in some places in strength, across Central Asia to the China Sea—this record makes it impossible to doubt the chances of such a mass movement as Kublai foretold. The Mongols were wavering. Their choice of a religion, as they ceased to be mere destroyers and settled

---

[1] Eileen Power, *Medieval People*, Pelican Books A 19, a sixpennyworth not to be missed; there is a splendid map, p. 48.
[2] A. C. Moule, *Christians in China before 1550*, pp. 136f.

down to become a state, was in the balance. Their own primitive nature-worship was falling away. As alternatives, they had met in their own territory Buddhism in the East, Islam in the West, Christianity thinly scattered over the whole. Which was it to be?

The opportunity was lost. It is easy to blame the Pope's preoccupation with European politics, especially the two-centuries-old struggle with Germany. If the Pope had been less an Italian Prince and more a statesman of the Kingdom of God he might have seen that here was the greatest chance in the whole history of the expansion of the Church. A later Pope, Nicholas IV, who had been General of the Franciscan Order, did in 1289 despatch missionaries to the Emperor Kublai Khan. They were late; the Mongols had begun to make another choice. They were few—a mere handful, never approaching the asked-for hundred. Most important of all, the Catholics who might have been as new blood infused into a decadent body, never got near, except in jealousy and strife, to the Nestorians who were before them in the field.

'So passed what may be described as the greatest might-have-been in the history of the Church. The Mongol or Turkish stock had been willing for a couple of generations to accept Christianity and not Islam as their national faith. . . . *Had it been presented to them by the oriental representatives of an undivided Christianity* there is little doubt that they would have done so. If this had happened, what might not have followed? '[1]

This is one of the points in history where one can

[1] W. A. Wigram, *The Assyrians and Their Neighbours*, p. 139 (italics mine).

hardly help going off into day-dreams. In the Near East the rule of the Turk might have been a blessing, not a curse, if his ancestors had chosen Christianity in the thirteenth century, instead of his waiting till our own time and then choosing only non-religious benefits of our way of life. Central Asia might not have been depopulated by that savage reversion to the nomad destroyer, Tamerlane; its surviving inhabitants might not have been for Christianity to-day the greatest closed area on the earth's surface, Moslem where it is not Bolshevik. China might not have been cut off from the Church's influence for two hundred years; and (since Moghul is but a re-writing of Mongol) the sixteenth-century conquerors of North India might have been Christian—and their descendants now. And all if two branches of the Church had been able to come together in united witness!

And 'a stumbling-block to the faithful'. A colleague in China conducted a mission, which was largely attended by students from the seven non-Christian colleges and universities of the city of Canton. He left a group of enquirers, men who had had no previous Christian connexion, in the charge of two keen and capable Chinese ministers. Weeks afterwards he found to his horror that the class had been allowed to melt away. They explained that the mission had been a Y.M.C.A. affair and they thought it might cause misunderstanding if they, ministers of the —— Church, stepped in to prepare these men for baptism. They had been brought up with such a healthy horror of sheep-stealing that it made them neglect to gather the lost sheep into any fold at all.

There you see what that Madras resolution means when it says:

'Co-operation in the great evangelistic task stops at the point where pastoral care is needed for the building up of the Church. We can act together in the presentation of the Gospel . . . but in the next necessary stage co-operation breaks down owing to divided church loyalty.'

The illustrations above are examples of that breakdown: comity—division of the territory among us so that we do not compete and overlap—was the reason which prevented that low-caste Indian tribe from coming over. Co-operation was the thing which seemed to make impossible pastoral care of converts of a joint mission. But there is another, and more positive, side to all this. It is not realized in the Older Churches how far we of the Younger have moved from anything like denominational isolation, moved by the pressure of common need. Consider:

A Quaker reproved John Wesley—

'because he found we were not led by the Spirit; for we fixed times of preaching beforehand: whereas we ought to do nothing, unless we were sensibly moved thereto by the Holy Ghost. . . . This was to regard the letter that killeth.'[1]

John, unrepentant, and, as often in controversy, unpacific, replied, 'God grant that I may so regard it all the days of my life!' I go regularly to a Quaker Meeting to preach. When first invited, I marvelled, remembering John: 'Do you have fixed times of

[1] *Journal*, 6th July 1739.

preaching? ' The answer is that it is a mission in a
city slum, with a mission service such as any one of
our churches would run in a similar environment. If
that is so when you move from the highly privileged,
and deeply pious circles to which many Friends have
always belonged, to a mission in a semi-pagan slum,
how much further has the process gone in foreign
missionary work! 'Meeting House'? That is what
all of us have to use in translating 'church' into the
Chinese language; there is no special evolution of a
sacred term like ἐκκλησία or κυριακὸν.[1] A ministry?
Friends have to have trained, professional, and
salaried staff, as much as any other mission. Silence
until the Spirit moves? No, you cannot do that with
the heathen who do not know what it is all about.
You must start further back.

Members of the Society of Friends will forgive me
for using them as a very obvious illustration. The
same is true of any one of our 'unhappy divisions'.
In so far as denominational distinctions represent a
negative reaction against abuses existing in the
Church as the Church then was in Europe, they are
meaningless except in the land of their origin. Even
there it may be true that some extremes have served
their purpose once the abuse which caused them has
passed into oblivion. It is not unfaithfulness if we
are moving from these distinctions towards a position
which is more *catholic*, i.e. more common—belonging
to that common heritage which lies beyond and
before our divisions.

---

[1] = 'the Lord's (house)', derivation of Anglo-Saxon *circe*
(church). *Ecclesia* is the word for the 'congregation' in the
Greek Old Testament.

Congregationalists—descendants, remember, of the Independents who believed in the autonomy of each local company of believers, and protested against the very idea of a national Church—form, next to Presbyterians, the main element in the Church of Christ in China, the most ambitious attempt at a national expression of Protestant Christianity. One Congregationalist missionary in India complained to me that something was going far wrong with one of the neighbouring churches. 'In the old days I, as a senior missionary, would have stepped in and put it right. But now, with the progress of devolution, it is another, and an Indian, minister's pastorate. We ought to have some central authority. . . .' ' A bishop? ' said I. ' You don't seem to me to be talking Congregationalism.' 'Congregationalism?' he replied. ' *They are not up to that yet.*' There is much to be said for his contention: some of our later forms of church order do imply a long training in something more elementary, more authoritarian. I know how the monarchical episcopate spread through the Early Church. I have known many monarchical *episcopoi* —Congregationalist, Baptist, Presbyterian and Methodist, as well as Anglican—ruling their churches with a firm and fatherly hand, as young churches need, and love, to be ruled.

The same is true of worship. The Madras findings say that the missionary of the future is to ' embody and transmit the experience of the Universal Church '. It goes on: ' To this end he should be familiar with types of worship other than those of his own church.'[1]

[1] *The Life of the Church*, Tambaram Madras Series, Vol. IV, p. 253.

I have been appalled at the results of transferring some worship traditions, away from the environment which produced them, to a young church in a non-Christian land. It has led to horrible irreverences when raw congregations have been led straight into ' free ' worship. No ingrained habits of reverence, no steeping in the devotions of the Psalter, no deep knowledge even of New Testament scriptures, no worthy hymn-book long contributing to the language of prayer, no experience of the discipline of a liturgy. The result too often is a meeting, with a ' chairman ', a little opening prayer—very little, because folk soon begin to shuffle and the main talk is not yet—noisy hymns, prelude to a long address; and if there is any-one who can do musical stunts, part of the meeting becomes a concert. To regard that as passing on one's worship tradition is surely to do injustice to one's spiritual ancestors.

We mistake our inheritance if we think of it only in terms of the negative reaction. To return to the Friends, as useful illustration : we think of Quaker worship as reaction against an abuse—against form which had been reduced to mere formalism. It was. But there was also a *positive* relation towards the past. Quaker worship meant passing on to another stage. Many non-Quakers would agree in saying ' to a higher stage ', because silent adoration, contempla-tion, and mental prayer are widely prized. But it is a stage which takes for granted the tradition pre-ceding it. What are you to do when there never has been a tradition preceding? Are you not in danger of starting in mid-air? Can you expect to feel in a pagan land, where it is the first or second century of the Church, as your forefathers did in seventeenth-century England?

At one time I was responsible for daily worship in a Chinese college chapel. I did not make them keep all the canonical hours, but morning and evening we used the sort of daily office in which medieval monks raised their souls to God. Some of my colleagues were surprised at this in a non-Anglican! But surely the conflicts of the past, and the consequent tenderness of some of our private feelings, must not be allowed to rob us of the Book of Common Prayer as the link by which we *all* are joined on to the Church of the West in its pre-Reformation period. The form of it, and most of the content, is from the medieval service books. Morning and Evening Prayer are from the Breviary—the book for the services at the eight canonical hours. In the prayer-book the eight services become two; English takes the place of Latin; it is for the ordinary congregation, not for the worship of monks. The medieval services consisted, and the two English services consist, mostly of the Psalter. In the monastery they went through the whole every week; in the parish church it takes a month. The varying Psalms and lessons are fitted into a permanent framework of prayers, responses, canticle, creed. When one remembers that the prayers are full of Biblical phrases, the responses are verses of the Psalms, the canticles are all from the Bible except *Te Deum* (which is itself strongly Biblical and undoubtedly inspired), and that the creed is merely a summary of Biblical facts, one realizes that this traditional form of public worship is more thoroughly scriptural than anything which has come to take its place. Why should not one—anyone—be free to return? At any rate I felt that I was standing for 'the experience of the Universal Church', and standing for it as that which fills up the negative aspects, corrects the partial emphases, of the narrower denominational position. I was explaining it thus to a visitor, when he re-marked, 'That's funny. In the field where my work is they do the liturgy beautifully. I am having to put all my energy into teaching *ex tempore* prayer.' I am a Methodist minister; my visitor was a distinguished member of one of the celibate orders of Anglo-Catholicism.

It is time we came together. I do not advocate the casting off of any positive denominational heritage. No scheme of Church union is worth considering which waters down every distinctive feature, so that there shall be nothing for anyone to object to. A Church so unified would contain nothing a man would die for either. . . . Church Reunion is not a least common denominator sum—it ought to be a grand addition.

But we cannot stop with the Younger Churches. How happy a fact it is that in China, for example, 61 per cent. of non-Roman Christians are linked to-gether in the National Christian Council. We have nothing to compare with that in our own land. They have comity instead of our competition, co-operation instead of our isolation; moreover it is on the mission field that schemes of reunion are taken seriously.

There, without realizing it, I was quoting their resolution again:

' We appeal with all the fervour we possess . . . to the

responsible authorities of the Older Churches to take this matter seriously to heart.'

That, I submit, with most churches here at home, has not begun to happen. How far has *Outline of a Re-union Scheme* affected denominational legislation? Are plans and policies one whit the less self-centred and self-regarding?

War came upon us in 1939, because from 1931 onwards (Japan's invasion of Manchuria) the nations failed to put collective security before individual interest. Are the churches in this regard any better than the nations?

For years there has been some talk of a United States of Europe. At first it moved only a minority of cranks. Then Federal Union became a catchword —and the title of a Penguin! Still it belonged to the idealists. Then came disaster. Without any preamble we heard one night, as though it were an announcement about pool petrol, that we had offered the French to pool the two Empires' resources and make a common citizenship. I am told that Bishop Gore once said of the Church's divisions that he did not know what would heal them ' unless very evil times force us together '. Behold the times!

Who is not impatient in these days with all partial memberships and partial ministries, all barriers to sacraments and to service? Who does not want to see the ministrations of all the churches at the disposal of everybody's need? If I were a chaplain, I should hate to pick out a few men from a company as ' mine '. Chaplains do not—at least not on active service, not in the front line. The fact is our

churches are trying to carry on their separate denominational lives at a time when no one knows
where the front line may be to-morrow. It may be
your own front street.

That to which we belong is the Church beyond
the churches. When shall we hear the call, match-
ing the need of the hour, to translate that consciousness of unity into worthier expression, ' that the
world may believe '?[1]

---

[1] A step which I suggest as immediately possible, and devoutly
to be wished, is the setting up of a National Christian Council of
Great Britain. The Younger Churches have been forced by the
pressure of need to act more sensibly long ago. Thus in China
there has been such a centre for joint work and witness since
1922. If we acknowledge the pressure of need which is upon us
now, the Older Churches may at last catch up with the Younger
in this regard.

The World Council of the Churches was being set up just before
the war. Surely, as the International Missionary Council has
presupposed a national consultative body in each land, so the
World Council could hardly work apart from some national
council to bring our scattered forces together.

PART II

THE HEROIC AGE IS COME AGAIN

CHAPTER IV

THE EARLY CHURCH AND THE YOUNGER CHURCHES

As a student of history I have lately been stirred with a deep discontent at failure to appreciate the significance of the modern missionary movement. If you are a medievalist you cannot neglect the Church. It is so central in society, so decisive in economics, so intertwined with political situations. Nothing is wholly secular. But take the *Cambridge Modern History*, which covers the period from the Renaissance down to *c.* 1900. Look up ' missionary ' in Volume XIII, the Index to the twelve which have gone before. You will find one reference, ' Missionary Ridge; fighting at, 1863.' It is an obscure place in Tennessee, scene of a skirmish during the American Civil War. Having drawn a blank there, try one of the great societies. I tried ' London Missionary Society '. This is more hopeful; the references are three. Two again concern, not battles, but minor incidents connected with the Boer War. The third looks more impressive. It occurs on a page where the headline runs, ' Niger problem solved —Livingstone.' But mistake it not: it is only the source of the *Niger River,* not the enlightening of the Dark Continent.

No one would expect preferential treatment of religion from the secular historian. But it is time to protest against a neglect of religious facts[1] which is itself a falsification of history. From 1792 onwards begins the Missionary Awakening. In England five of the great societies are founded within ten years. Within fifty all the foremost missionary agencies of the British Isles, of the Protestant churches of the Continent of Europe, and of the United States of America, are in the field. In the Roman communion missionary zeal revives and reaches an unprecedented pitch. There begins an expansion of the Church which is unequalled in any page of history. The *Cambridge Modern History* gives a whole volume to the French Revolution, and another to Napoleon. But there is no mention of that contemporary movement which is the greatest happening since Pentecost.

We of the churches are victims of this falsification. Congregations think of overseas missions as a special charity, like the hospitals—but more distant and peculiar—for which funds are raised as one of the Church's side-lines. Ministers regard missions as a sphere of work which drew the more romantic of their fellow theologues, whence they return to tell amusing anecdotes of the strange ways of the heathen, or sobstuff stories of his conversion, according to taste. Even in our programme of theological studies you may see it: my own chair was almost called ' Church History and the History of Missions '.

[1] I am neither overlooking nor disparaging the valuable Volume II on the Reformation, nor such occasional sections as the chapter by Gwatkin on Religious Toleration in Volume V, and the (scanty) ten pages given by Temperley to the revival in the eighteenth century in Volume VI.

I objected, and I still object. Missions are not an added extra. This thing is the life of the Church.

With this in mind, examine the course of Church History: the urge of essential Christianity in the Apostolic Age carries the Church forward in an expansion which lasts three hundred years, until the Roman world submits, and the Galilean has conquered. Then through the long centuries of the Middle Ages, some of them dark, many of them dull, there are repeated revivals of the spirit of essential Christianity. The typical medieval expression of revival is a monastic movement. And the monks are the medieval missionaries.[1] You are reminded of this connexion between revival, monk, mission, by St. Benedict, the framer of that Rule which decided the form to be taken by monasticism in the whole of the West. The first Benedictine house to be established away from the Roman environment where the movement began, was that mission station of Augustine's at Canterbury. Europe was converted by monks. They were equally prominent in the Greek Church in its advance in North Africa and its entry into Russia. It was Persian monks who first took the gospel across Asia to the Far East (635).

The most significant of the later revivals is that which found expression in the Friars. This is a revival which still warms our hearts, especially as we see it in the Little Poor Man of Assisi. St. Francis marks the re-emergence of missions into the Church of the later Middle Ages. He himself preaches before the Sultan of Egypt—when other Christians

[1] J. T. Addison, *The Medieval Missionary*.

express their zeal only by fighting the Saracen.
Others go to Morocco: ' Now I can truly say that I
have five real brothers,' says the Saint when he hears
of their martyrdom.   Still more go to Persia, into
the lands of the Mongols, and on to India and the
Far East.

The Reformation is a revival (some would say *the*
revival) of essential Christianity. It was robbed of its
natural counterpart, resumption of the missionary
task, by the sad fact that Protestants had a long
struggle for existence.   It was so long that they used
up their energies in self-defence, and settled into an
attitude of self-regarding.   This is a fair sample of
the Protestant mind:

' To spread abroad the knowledge of the Gospel among
barbarous and heathen nations seems to be highly pre-
posterous. . . . Whilst there remains at home a single
individual without the means of religious knowledge, to
propagate it abroad would be improper and absurd.'[1]

But there was one part of the sixteenth-century
revival, ill-called the counter-Reformation (as though
it had only negative significance!), which enabled
the Church of Rome to claim the New World, and
the new routes across the Old World, for Christ.
Such an expansion of Christianity takes place then as
has in all the centuries before never been witnessed.[2]

Finally comes the Evangelical Revival of the
eighteenth century, which quickens the life of every
communion in the British Isles.   There is a contemporary revival, the Great Awakening, doing the
same for North America.   The continent of Europe

---

[1] General Assembly of the Church of Scotland, 1796.
[2] Latourette, *A History of the Expansion of Christianity*, III, 52.

has already been stirred by the earlier movements of Pietists and Moravians. And lo, we are in it, belated, but not too late. The greatest missionary movement of all the Church's history has begun.[1] It still proceeds—as I have said, the greatest event since Pentecost.

Missions are the life of the Church, the expression of essential Christianity. Whenever the Church revives, it is to become again the Church preaching the gospel to every creature.

Having made these two points, (1) that the Church is essentially a missionary Church, and (2) that the modern missionary movement is the biggest event since Pentecost, let me make another which fits them both together, and really illumines the whole subject of missions as nothing else does: (3) The Younger Churches are the Early Church of our day.

It is obvious once it is stated. We all recognize in the great missionary pioneers apostolic figures. We have been slower to realize that those (how did we dub them?) 'more romantic' fellow theologues who went to the mission field have anything like that significance, men of the sub-apostolic age; that the struggling churches which they seek to serve are the Early Church come to life again; that there is hardly a problem, a situation, a task, belonging to the history of the Church in the first four centuries which is not a chief preoccupation to the men of the missionary movement to-day.

It is of vital importance that missionaries, ministers, and members of the Younger Churches should come to this realization. They are not facing

[1] *Ibid.*, 457.

problems for the first time. They are rich in the
treasury of experience. They stand alongside saints
and fathers in a Church with a heroic past. There
is only one thing that matters nearly as much. It is
that you of the Church at home should know what
you are doing when you stand in with us on the
missionary task. You are not patronizing one of the
side-lines, turning from the Church's main, though
humdrum, work to a refreshing romanticism. You
are claiming and making real your relationship to:

> ' The glorious company of the apostles . . .
> The goodly fellowship of the prophets . . .
> The noble army of martyrs . . .
> The holy Church throughout all the world.'

It would make a difference to missionary education,
missionary prayer-meetings, missionary giving, the
flow of missionary candidates, if you of the Older
Churches believed that.

Of course you realize that the local church in the
early centuries is often not a very impressive affair.
Celsus describes a typical group of the Christians
whom he despises:

' Workers in wool, and leather, laundrymen, and persons of the most uneducated and rustic character, who
would not venture to utter a word in the presence of their
elders or of their wiser masters. . . .'[1]

But, he adds, what a gabbling goes on when they
are alone, or when they get hold of someone as un-
instructed as themselves! I have seen just such.
You may see them in any group of reclaimed out-

[1] Origen, *Contra Celsum*, iii, 55.

castes or of low-caste Christians in South India. Leather-workers and dhobies are despised there too. Just like those slaves of the Roman Empire, these offscourings of Indian society steal away to the meeting of that new community where their serfdom is forgotten. There these base ones take on a new dignity. Celsus' wool-worker is perhaps a catechist; the tanner a reader of the Scriptures; the voice which has echoed through the laundry may lead in the singing of the hymns. They enter a different world, where they are no more slaves of the household of Junius and Andronicus—or shall we say chattels of the landlord of Travancore or Hyderabad?—but sons and daughters of the household of God. 'Called Christians by the vulgar,' says Tacitus. It sounds very much like what a Chinese intellectual would say if he followed you in to see the rather ill-ordered worship of a Chinese congregation; shopmen and coolies, working women, and old grannies so nearly illiterate that they have to follow the reading of the prayer-book with a finger on each character, and even so they are half a sentence behind. 'I find nothing in it,' says Pliny, the enlightened governor of Bithynia, writing to the Emperor Trajan, 'nothing but a debased superstition carried to great extremes.' He had been questioning under torture 'two women who were called deaconesses'. They were not the stuff to impress him much. Biblewomen, we should call them now.

Fortunately a booklet[1] has survived which may be similar to that used by the 'wool-worker' of Celsus'

---

[1] The *Didache*, or *Teaching of the Twelve Apostles*. S.P.C.K. have an edition which costs only 3d.

obscure group, or by the 'deaconesses' of Pliny's persecution, in preparing a candidate for baptism. Let us see what religious education was like at the beginning of the second century:

First we shall notice that it is intensely practical. It does not begin with 'Who made you?—God made me,' like one catechism I know; nor yet with 'What are the names of the Trinity?' like one catechist I heard in China. It begins:

> 'There are Two Ways: one of Life, the other of Death.
> The Way of Life is . . .'

Christianity is not so much concerned with how your life began as with how it begins anew; not so much with correct theology as with that experience which is prior to all theology.

Then follow the three commandments of our Lord: 'Thou shalt love God who made thee'—ah, that is better than 'Who made you?'—'Thou shalt love thy neighbour as thyself,' and the Golden Rule in its negative form. Commentary follows which is largely quotation from the Sermon on the Mount.

The next part may be described as the Ten Commandments Up-to-date. The words of Exodus are not slavishly reproduced. There is, for example, nothing about keeping the seventh day, because they are not going to, being Christians, not Jews. There are additions, expansions, illustrations of the spirit of Old Testament morality in terms of life in the contemporary Roman Empire: Not only 'Thou shalt not steal,' but 'Thou shalt not use magic.' Not only 'Thou shalt not commit adultery,' but 'Thou shalt not

procure abortion nor kill the new-born child.' These
are things already condemned among the Hebrews,
but, as to-day, ghastly commonplaces in the pagan
society which surrounds Gentile converts. Along
with false witness, we find condemned slander,
malice, and a double tongue. Instead of going into
the rigmarole about 'his ox nor his ass' it adds to
the warning against covetousness:

'Thou shalt not be extortionate, nor a hypocrite, nor
spiteful, nor arrogant. Thou shalt not take evil counsel
against thy neighbour. Thou shalt hate no man, but
some thou shalt reprove, and for some thou shalt pray,
and some thou shalt love better than thine own soul.'

Then comes tender advice—each section beginning
with, 'My child'—dwelling on the Christian virtues,
and meant to direct the man's new life as a humble,
patient, trustful child of God:

'The accidents that befall thee, thou shalt welcome as
good, knowing that without God nothing cometh to pass.'

Next is teaching about the Church—again not
theory, but practice, church-*going*. You must go;
you cannot be a Christian without:

'My child, night and day shalt thou remember him
that speaketh the word of God to thee, and thou shalt
honour him as the Lord.'

There is a lofty view of the Christian ministry
which needs to be taught in the Younger Churches
now—remember him night and day, because of his
tremendous responsibility, and of your soul's depen-
dence upon him. 'Daily shalt thou seek the faces

of the saints,' that is, of the other Christians. This
new community is to be a real thing. And there are
to be no squabbles : ' Thou shalt not seek division.'
When troubles do arise, you shall vote on the side
of justice, not partisanship. And you shall be ready
to communicate to the needs of others. Christians
stand together—if partners in eternal things, how
much more in the things that perish. Religious
education for the home is here too : you must bring
up your children in this way. If you are masters,
religion must make you treat your slaves differently.
If you are slaves, you must show a new regard for
your masters. Keep these commandments, and when
you fail, make your confession ' in the congregation '.

One who has done valuable pioneer work in com-
paring the Early Church and the work of modern
missions, criticizes the level of Christian life which
he finds common to post-apostolic literature, and to
his experiences in China and Korea.[1] It is, he says,
a legalism, which misses the depths of St. Paul's
mystical experience, salvation by grace through faith.
It is a new morality and little more. With regard to
the *Didache* I believe it is true, with regard to the
Younger Churches I feel it may be, that the necessary moral emphasis escapes the danger if it is made
within the concept of a sacramental life, whose portal
is Baptism, the experience of a new birth, making
the new morality possible even for a poor child of
sin; a life which is constantly fed by communion
with the saints, and especially by that which comes
to be called *the* communion, the Eucharist.

So here we are, with the candidate at the river-

[1] Campbell N. Moody, *The Mind of the Early Converts.*

side. You may see the sight nowadays, on the banks of the Ganges or the Godaveri. It is an ideal spot, because 'living' (i.e. flowing) water is to be preferred to still. But there are already provisions, soon to increase as Christianity passes beyond lands where ablutions in the river are considered natural and right, which even in the *Didache* make baptism by sprinkling permissible. Here the catechumen takes his vows. The church joins in prayer for him. He steps down into the river. He is born into newness of life, enters upon this new world, as they all have done before him. No more a child of sin, he too is one of the elect race, the royal priesthood, the holy nation.[1] He is 'washed', as Justin says,[2] 'in the name of the Father, Son and Holy Ghost, as we learned from the Apostles'. Or he is 'illumined'—brought out of darkness into His marvellous light.

Thus from the riverside they bring him back into the town to the church meeting. Here we may notice a difference. The Apostles knew no church buildings, and the post-apostolic Church continued thus till the end of the second century. In the Roman Empire the Church was an illicit society, with no right to hold property. But this proved no great disability; most Christians were householders, and they continued the New Testament tradition of 'the church which is in the house'.[3] In Jewish buildings the meeting-place was an upper guest-room, con-

---

[1] 1 Peter ii. 9.

[2] *Apology*, written c. 150. See especially I, 65-67.

[3] For the Jerusalem church see Luke xxii. 12, Acts i. 13, ii. 46, v. 42, xii. 12, which I take to refer to the same house. For house-churches among the Gentiles see Romans xvi. 5, 23, 1 Corinthians xvi. 19, Colossians iv. 15, Philemon 2.

veniently reached by an outside stair. With Gentiles
it would be the hall or reception room (*atrium*), the
place where for pagans the altar to the household
gods would stand. Many of us have been at similar
gatherings—a new cause where 'kinsmen and near
friends' are called in and waiting for the missionary,
just like the household of Cornelius at Caesarea.[1] But
with our greater freedom—sometimes *too* great
haste in saddling a young church with property—
long before our 'post-apostolic age' we have rented
a shop in the village street, or put up a gospel hall
in the town.

The service consists of the reading of the Old Testament Scriptures, 'the memoirs of the Apostles' as
Justin calls the Gospels, and doubtless an occasional
letter which survives from the first missionaries—the
Epistles; preaching—it may be by the local pastor,[2]
or by some visiting 'prophet' (which seems to be the
name for the successors of those pioneer missionaries
known to the previous generation as Apostles)—'he
exhorts us', says Justin, 'to imitation of these good
things'; and prayers—'we rise to pray'—for themselves, for the newly baptized, for all men everywhere,
for a good life, and for everlasting salvation. Pliny's
letter tells the Emperor that 'they sing antiphonally
to Christ as to a god', and of course we know that
not only the Psalms but early Christian hymns have
come down to us in the Scriptures.[3]

[1] Acts x. 24.
[2] Justin calls him 'president'. Church order is only in process
of formation at this time. But it may be that he uses this word
because he writes for outsiders who are not used to the Church's
peculiar terms.
[3] See article 'Hymns' in *Dictionary of the Apostolic Church*.

The first part of the service ends with the kiss of peace:[1] Justin says, 'When we have concluded the prayers we salute one another with a kiss,' the family greeting which, as Acts and Epistles bear witness, was from the beginning adopted by this close community, this real family of the children of God. Having the privilege to be present at the Eucharist of one branch of the ancient Syrian Church in South India, I found that at the end of their pre-communion they retain this apostolic custom—sensibly modified to fit Indian, or indeed any, society. The celebrant takes the deacon's hands between his own, and then the deacon does the same to the worshipper at the end of each row, and so the hand-clasp is passed round the church. I mention it to contrast this strong community emphasis of primitive Christianity with the individualist spirit of worship as most of us know it. Then begins the Eucharist itself: 'Bread and wine are brought to the president.' It is he, pastor of the local flock, who normally celebrates. The 'prophet' (itinerant missionary), says the *Didache*, is also to be allowed. In the second century there are no missionary societies to select candidates, and so it is left to the local churches, and their rulers—which means their regularly appointed ministry—to select true from false among those whom a missionary call has set wandering over the world as His witnesses. This has already become a real and pressing problem.[2]

Having received the elements, the celebrant leads in praise and thanksgiving, 'and all the people express their assent by saying Amen'. The deacons distri-

[1] See article 'Salutations' in *Dictionary of the Apostolic Church*.
[2] See, e.g. *Didache*, xi, about testing a prophet.

bute the elements and carry to those who are absent.
' Eucharist ' (thanksgiving), explains Justin, is the
name given to the food, which, ' blessed by the prayer
of the Word ', becomes the Saviour's flesh and blood.
The ' Word ' surely means here our Lord's words of
institution. That which is central is the repetition of
the act of our Lord. Indeed that is the only fixed
part of the Eucharist. The prayers, Justin implies,
are free, though models are early begun.[1] It would
be easy to pick out from second-century literature
extravagant phrases which seem to imply magical
conceptions of the Church's sacraments. In the
Younger Churches we know how hard it is to shake
off our pagan ancestors! But here in Justin and the
Didache are great moral emphases: It is, says Justin,
for none but believers, who have been baptized and
are regenerate, ' and who so live as Christ has
directed '. The *Didache* adds that confession has
preceded:

' . . . after confessing your transgressions, that your sacrifice may be pure, but let none who has a quarrel with
his fellow join in your meeting till they be reconciled,
that your sacrifice be not defiled.'

There you see how far back reach those words of our
office:

' Ye therefore that do truly and earnestly repent of
your sins and are in love and charity with your neighbours . . .'

Justin says it is something which ' afterwards we
always remind each other of, and the wealthy among

[1] *Didache*, ix.

us help the needy, and we always keep together'.
The offerings are deposited with the 'president' for
'orphans, widows, the sick, the poor, those in bonds,
and the strangers among us'.

Read the eucharistic prayers of *Didache*, ix. The
two thanksgivings, over the cup and over the bread,
are difficult in one respect but significant in another.
They bear no mention of our Lord's passion, but
they are full of this sense of community—of being
in Him, who is the Vine while we are the branches,
of being united to one another, like the bread,

'scattered upon the mountains, but brought together,
and become one. So let Thy Church be gathered together from the ends of the earth into Thy Kingdom, for
Thine is the glory and the power through Jesus Christ
for ever.'

It all emphasizes that which throughout is tremen-
dously important. A modern missionary is tempted
sometimes to think that religion in a young church
is too much a matter of attendance at meetings—
often rather ill-conducted meetings. But it is in line
with apostolic tradition.

'Be frequently gathered together seeking the things
that belong to your souls. . . . We always keep together.
. . . My child, night and day remember him that
speaketh the word of God to thee. . . . Afterwards we
always remind one another of these things.'

Their meetings may not seem much, but they are
all they have got, and represent all that they are.
Most hours of the day are spent in the pagan society
of a wicked world. Here they become, and know
themselves to be, the nucleus of that new people of

God, which is the crown of His creation. Of course they must come together, keep together, remind one another.

Their numbers increased. At the end of the second century Tertullian is able to claim:

> 'We are of yesterday, yet we have filled everything of yours—cities, tenements, villages, towns, markets, even camps, tribes, town-councils, palace, senate, forum; we have left to you only the temples.'[1]

After careful weighing of the evidence, Harnack agrees that the period after Commodus (d. 192) 'saw Christianity a serious factor in the provinces and throughout the Empire'.[2] He finds it still more amazing that so early as this same period the non-Christian world should recognize Christians as 'the third race': 'Plane, tertium genus dicimur.'[3] Roman polytheists, Jews, and Christians, that is the order.

At about the same stage in its progress, according to the measure of time, men of the 'Early Church' to-day might make their boast as boldly as Tertullian. For ten years we have seen the number of the Church's adherents (not counting the Roman communion) in lands of the Younger Churches advance by half a million a year.[4] The third race? In India parliamentary representation has been introduced on a communal basis. In Japan religious bodies have been forced to register under government. In both countries this has meant recognition of Christianity as the third community—a sign of success not with-

---

[1] *Apology*, xxxvii.
[2] *Mission and Expansion of Christianity*, I, 32.
[3] Tertullian, *Ad Nationes*, i, 8; Harnack, op. cit., I, 275.
[4] *Interpretative Statistical Survey of the World Mission*, p. 18.

out its embarrassments because of the political implications.[1] As for Christianity's being 'a serious factor in the provinces', in China so long ago as 1912 one could turn from the undistinguished congregation mentioned above, and remember that in Kwangtung 65 per cent. of the provincial officials were the product of Christian schools, and that in Peking three cabinet ministers were professing Christians.

Indeed one's thoughts may with justice leave the age of Tertullian and go on to the Christian Empire. In the middle of the seventeenth century, at the downfall of the Ming dynasty, Jesuit priests baptized the son of the fugitive Emperor, and gave him the name of Constantine. They hoped that the throne might be regained and he become the first Christian Emperor of Rome's eastern counterpart. That was not to be. But a triumph not dissimilar to that of the fourth century, except indeed in the depth of the experience of conversion, is to be seen in the General-issimo and his lady, and their open patronage of the Christian cause to-day.

How did the faith spread? Celsus gives us a picture of that too. 'They get hold of young people and certain women as ignorant as themselves. They pour out wonderful statements.' The gist of them is : Take no notice of your father or your teachers. We alone know the right way to live. We will show you how to be happy and to make your home happy. The conversation is interrupted by the approach of some-one of real authority, so they give a parting invitation, ' " Come with the women and your playmates to the

[1] Next to Hinduism and Islam in India; next to Sect Shinto and Buddhism in Japan.

women's apartments, or the leather shop, or the
laundry. There you may attain to the perfect life! "
With such words they win them over.'[1]

He means it to be a sinister picture of ignorant
busybodies disturbing the peace of a household.
But some of us as we read think with affection of
similar humble witnesses whom we know. Let those
barely literate women of an Eastern congregation
to-day get an opening into any home, and they will
be there, regularly and in turn, to read the Scriptures
in the women's apartments. If the church gets one
of a family its members do not let go until the
family is Christian. I know a barber's shop in a
Chinese city where during a haircut the assistant
told me, 'We too have an opportunity to hear the
gospel. The proprietor is a Christian.' I know a
restaurant where the master led twenty of his young
waiters to Christian baptism on one day.[2] I know
a hotel where the Christian management makes a
point of having a Bible in every bedroom. Above
all, I think of one Chinese friend who told me,
'There is always somebody I'm after!' It is still
true that by such devices they win them over.

Of course there was opposition—was, and is.
More men have suffered martyrdom for the Lord
Jesus during these last twenty-five years than in all
the heroic centuries to which we look back as to the
Church's golden age. The same spirit which has
been the glory of Western Christendom has re-
appeared, true to type, in every land wheresoever
the Church has been planted. The only considerable

---

[1] Origen, *Contra Celsum*, iii, 55.
[2] My *Chinese Church in Action*, pp. 110ff.

national delegation absent from the Madras Meeting was that of Manchuria: they could not get passports. Indeed many Christian leaders had lost their liberty. Not a few have laid down their lives. That is one example.

I sat next to an ordinary-looking young man during one session at Madras. He shocked me by prefacing some statement with the words, 'A few weeks ago when I came out of prison . . .' I glanced at his name-card, turned him up in my *Who's Who* —a young Turk from Chinese Turkestan. The eastward spread of the power of the Soviets has added this to the tale of territories where Christians are driven out, or driven into the catacombs. That is the second type of modern persecution.

I can tell little of first-hand experience among the confessors and holy martyrs of these days, but I do know something of the apologists. I was working among students in China during the Anti-Christian Movement of 1925-8. Here extremes of nationalism and communism combined.[1]

'We especially oppose Christianity because of:
    Science: evolution, astronomy, psychology, and physiology destroy belief in creation and immortality.
    Morals: the doctrine of redemption encourages sin. . . .
    Nationalism: Christianity is the vanguard of imperialism and a means of exploitation.'

They were even clever enough to pick up bits of imported Biblical criticism and hurl our own prob-

[1] See my *Chinese Realities*, pp. 134-159, for further translations of their propaganda.

lems at us for our greater confusion. It seemed to
young Christians a dreadfully formidable attack, so
new and unexpected to those who had regarded
themselves, and been regarded, as pioneers of progress, morality, and patriotism. I was able to turn
up charges made by second-century anti-Christian
writers.[1] Christianity was unscientific—'Certain of
them do not wish either to give or receive reasons
for those things which they hold—they say, Do
not examine, only believe!' Christianity was im-
moral—'Whoever, they say, is a sinner . . . him
will the Kingdom of God receive. . . . Whom else
would a man invite if he were making proclamation
for a band of robbers?' Christianity denationalized
—'They have forsaken their national rites for the
Law of Christ.' Yes, even Biblical criticism—'Is it
Moses who lied, or Jesus? Did the Father . . . forget
. . . or did He change His mind, and condemning
His own laws send forth a messenger with the
opposite instructions?' There it is, the whole lot
of it, not something formidable and new, but a
failure eighteen centuries old! And in that spirit
we began to face our critics with confidence, and
with a smile.

Besides opposition from one or other of modern
extremist ideologies, there is opposition from the
religions which Christianity seeks to dispossess.
When from Jerusalem in 1928 men looked out upon
the non-Christian religions of the world, they saw
old spiritual homes breaking up, unable to stand
against the pressure of modern life. Increasingly it

[1] The quotations which follow are all extracts from *Contra Celsum*.

was becoming a question of either the Christian religion or no religion. 'Madras 1938' came to different findings. We saw old religions taking on new strength. Often this is by alliance with national, racial, or *volk* feeling: such is the case with Hinayana Buddhism in Ceylon, Burma, and Thailand; with Hinduism; and with the young Moslem who thus forcibly expressed himself, 'I don't give a damn for the Koran, but I'd die for the Moslem community.'

Another factor is that many non-Christian religions have been leavened by Christian influences, and have come consciously to copy Christian ways. They sing 'How sweet the name of Buddha sounds', start a Y.M.B.A., a hospital of the red swastika, a Buddhist evangelistic campaign, tracts, magazines, and wireless broadcasts. Hindus preach Christian ideals, but read them back into their own *Vedas*, to show that India has no need of Christ. Even changeless Islam has had to translate its Arabic scriptures into the languages of the people in order to compete with the Bible Societies.

But it has all happened before. The Emperor Julian, whom Christians know as the Apostate[1] (361-3), called to the peoples of the Roman Empire to 'worship the gods rightly and justly in the manner transmitted to us from the most ancient times'. Paganism was extolled as worship of 'gods of your forefathers', Christianity dismissed as 'servitude to the despisers of your national rites'.

[1] Good examples of the writings of Julian may be found in B. J. Kidd, *Documents Illustrative of the History of the Church*, II, 50-66; also in the lengthy article in *Dictionary of Christian Biography*.

Still more striking a parallel is Julian's attempt
to revitalize paganism. Attention must be paid,
he says, to the means whereby 'irreligion' (i.e.
Christianity) has spread—'humanity to strangers,
care in burying the dead, pretended sanctity of life'.
Priests must begin to attend temple worship with
their wives and children and servants, stop going
to licentious shows, break their associations with
charioteers and dancers. They must not truckle to
dignitaries, but treat a nobleman as a private individual once he enters the temple. Julian may call it
'*pretended* sanctity', but here is sound testimony
to family life, morality, and spiritual independence
among the Christian clergy!

'Erect hospitals in every city,' he says, 'that strangers
may partake of our benevolence; and not only those of
our own religion, but others also.'

This is explained with surprising candour:

'None of the Jews beg, and the impious Galileans
relieve both their own poor and ours.'

But these virtues he, too, seeks to read back into
his Homer:

'Accustom them to acts of kindness, and teach them
that this was the old way.'

Thus he adopted for paganism, says Gregory of
Nazianzus, schools, preaching, lectures both moral
and doctrinal, a liturgy, the penitential system, the
catechumenate and baptism, hostels for pilgrims,
monasteries, charity, letters of introduction for

travellers, 'things which he had especially admired in our institutions'.[1]

Paganism has vanished in the West—at least until its recent German revival. The only lasting significance of Julian's attempt to re-establish it is that he thus provides, in a century when there are many evidences of the spread of a merely nominal Christianity, the best testimony to the Church's widespread influence, incomparable standards, and capacity to endure.

With regard to the revival of paganism in modern Europe, one may be forgiven recalling the story of a scoffer of Julian's time: 'What,' said he, 'is your Carpenter doing now?' Said the unperturbed Christian, 'Making a coffin for your Emperor!' We may well be thankful that we belong to the *historic* Church, especially if for us, through our fellowship with the Younger Churches, Church History has come to life.[2]

---

[1] *Orationes*, iv, 111.
[2] Other subjects suggest themselves for comparison: See my article in *The Life of the Church*, Tambaram Madras Series, Vol. IV, pp. 258ff. Here two will follow: The great subject of Church and State—including the reappearance of Emperor worship in the Japanese Empire—follows in Chapter V. Chapter VI will deal with second-century Gnosticism and attempts at ' indigenous expression ' now.

EMPEROR WORSHIP—THEN AND NOW

' " Render unto Caesar the things that are Caesar's and unto God the things that are God's." And so it is only to God that we make obeisance (προσκυνοῦμεν), while to you we gladly do service in other ways, acknowledging you kings and rulers of men, and praying that with kingly might you may be found to have also a judgment which is sound. But if you disregard our prayers . . .'

THAT, from the first *Apology* of Justin,[1] is one of the great 'buts' in the history of the Church. It is worthy in the new dispensation of being put alongside Daniel iii. 17, 18, in the old:

' Our God whom we serve is able to deliver us ' (said Shadrach, Meshach, and Abed-nego) ' but if not . . .'

As under Nebuchadnezzar in Babylon, as in the revived State-worship of imperial Rome, again in our day Caesar lays claim to that which can properly belong only to God. 'Church and State': the phrase makes us think of the cult of the State in Nazi Germany and Fascist Italy. Some of us go on to think of our own hopes, vague yet and unexpressed (unless the launching of the World Council of the Churches just before the war be a beginning of such

[1] xvii.

84

expression), hopes of a new order rising out of the present ruin, where Christian people shall find a loyalty transcending the international anarchy. . . . 'Church and State' is no foreign problem, far removed. While bearing in mind its relevance here, we shall consider chiefly one part of the Universal Church which is perhaps far removed, but which is facing this problem in its most acute form, and which in Christian charity demands our understanding and our prayers. As a teacher of Church History I am always trying to persuade people that the Younger Churches are (as indeed one might have expected) repeating some of the tremendous experiences of the Early Church. Nowhere in the world is there so clear a case for comparison of the modern crisis and the ancient conflict as in the Japanese Empire.

Anyone entering Japanese territory has, added to the usual horrors of customs declarations, the task of making a list of all his books, with the name of the author of each, for police inspection. So carefully does the State seek to guard its people against the invasion of 'dangerous thoughts'. In the days when new missionaries were going out—before that turn in the tide which now seems to be bringing them home again—I used to tell my students that I hoped their list would include some of the *Acta Martyrum*, *Apologies* like that of Justin and the still more outspoken one of Tertullian, other writings of the heroic period of the Church from the Book of the Revelation onwards. The inspector would not make a fuss about any of these—unless indeed one were so conscientious as to omit the author's name in the case of The Revelation! He would not see their relevance.

But the young missionary would. For to enter Japanese territory is to step back over the centuries to a land where Emperor worship is a living reality, and may at any time become a challenge confronting the Church.

Of course we must not assume that they are exactly parallel cases, or we shall prejudge the issue. But the trouble so far seems rather to have been that those who have provided material to help us make our judgment have done so apart from the background of history. It is always a mistake to act as though either human wisdom or divine guidance were beginning anew with ourselves. As Christians we must take into account the centuries of experience to which we are rightful heirs.

The very fussiness of the police already mentioned will remind you of the parallel. In the Roman capital too the police system was thorough and efficient, keeping especial watch over (technically illicit) *collegia*.[1] From the provinces, governors sent reports which are striking for the minute recording of all that might possibly affect the security of the State. If in every meeting in Japan there is the police spy, it was the same fear of 'dangerous thoughts' which caused Roman Emperors to ban the most innocent of societies. Pliny was thinking of founding something like an Auxiliary Fire Service in the city of Nicomedeia. Trajan wrote back:

'Whatever name they bear, it is almost certain that men so united will become a political club. It will be better therefore to supply the necessary apparatus in case of fire, to warn the landlords to take precautions for

[1] E. G. Hardy, *Christianity and the Roman Government*, pp. 47f.

themselves, and in case of necessity to make use of the populace in extinguishing the flames.'[1]

Give them the stirrup-pumps and leave them to it! Fires are not so fearful as dangerous thoughts!

The year 248 was kept in Rome as the thousandth anniversary of the founding of the city, by the twins Romulus and Remus, sons by a human mother of Mars, the god of war. The year 1940 was kept in Japan as the two thousand six hundredth anniversary of the foundation of the Empire by Jimmu Tennō, who was the great-grandchild of Ninigi-no-Mikoto, who was the grandson of Amaterasu-Omikami, the goddess of the Sun.[2] If you do a little sum you will see that both legendary beginnings are within the same century. Both celebrations were somewhat overcast. In Rome it was a period of decline, as anyone could see. The festival falls almost exactly in the middle of a period of seventy years when the Empire was ruled by the 'barrack-room Emperors'. There were twenty-three in all—that means an average reign of three years. Most of these military despots met a violent death at a rival's hands. In Japan it was the time when long-laid plans of imperial expansion on the mainland of Asia ought to have been realized. A desperate attempt was made to finish off the 'China incident' so that the Emperor might have a worthy report to make at the Grand Imperial Shrine of Ise. But the 'incident' dragged on, a steady drain of blood and treasure, a wound which would not heal.

Origen saw what was likely to result: Rome was

[1] Quoted by T. R. Glover in *Christ in the Ancient World*, p. 31.
[2] D. C. Holtom, *The National Faith of Japan*, p. 132.

in decline because the gods were angry; the gods of Rome were angry because they were neglected; they were neglected because Christians had for a generation been left to undisturbed progress:

' It is likely that the secure existence, as regards this world, enjoyed by believers now, will come to an end, since those who in every way slander the Word put down the present frequency of sedition to the crowd of believers, and to their not being warred against by the leaders as in the old days.'[1]

The advocates of renewed persecution were right at least in this—it had been the time of rapid growth in numbers.[2] Indeed it is in the writings of Origen that we find a confidence which, in spite of the high-sounding boasts of earlier Apologists—'We have left to you only the temples,' says Tertullian about the year 200—must be accounted new. After the forty years of peace (210-250), there appears, instead of the earlier idea of a not too long delayed destruction of this wicked world, the hope of the world's conversion. It has become the fashion with some recently to speak as though any this-worldly realization of the Kingdom of God were part of the discredited optimism of nineteenth-century liberalism. But what of this from the third century, not the nineteenth?

' It is evident that even the barbarians, when they yield obedience to the word of God, will become most obedient to the law, and most humane; and every form of worship will be destroyed except the religion of Christ, which will

---

[1] *Contra Celsum*, iii, 15.
[2] A. Harnack, *The Mission and Expansion of Christianity*, II, 10-17.

alone prevail. And indeed it will one day triumph, as its
principles take possession of the minds of men more and
more every day. . . . And what are we to expect, if not
only a very few agree, as at present, but the whole of the
Empire of Rome?

'. . . If all the Romans . . . embrace the Christian
faith . . . they will not war at all. . . . For men of God
are assuredly the salt of the earth: they preserve the
order of the world. . . .

'Afterwards he (Celsus) says: "If it were possible,"
implying that he thought it most desirable, "that all the
inhabitants of Asia, Europe, and Libya, Greeks and Barbarians, all to the uttermost ends of the earth, were
to come under one law . . . Anyone who thinks this
possible, knows nothing." It would require careful consideration and lengthened argument to prove that it is
not only possible, but certain, that all who are endowed
with reason will come under one law.'[1]

Here we have left the hard sayings of Jewish
apocalyptic, and have the Kingdom interpreted in
terms of its coming triumph in—and even beyond—
the Roman Empire.

In Japan the ten years ending in 1935 have seen
an advance of 55 per cent. in the number of
communicants of non-Roman churches.[2] Kagawa
estimates that the rate of increase has gone far
towards being doubled.[3] The 'Kingdom of God
Movement' led by him in the years after the
Jerusalem Meeting of 1928 played no small part in
this. Growth in numbers meant growth in influence.
And this brought increased attention from the
Government. Mention of 'Jerusalem 1928' reminds

---

[1] *Contra Celsum*, viii, 68-70; see also iii, 29, 54; viii, 59.
[2] *Interpretative Statistical Survey of the World Mission.*
[3] *Christ and Japan*, p. 124.

us of another factor: increasingly the Ecumenical Movement demonstrates the supra-national nature of the Church. The proposal to hold the next (1938) Meeting of the International Missionary Council in China caught the critical eye of Japanese officialdom. If in Asia, why not in Japan? In any case international relationships are not a recommendation to any government which seeks to develop extremes of national feeling. Thus came the startling events of the autumn of 1940: The Salvation Army in Japan was forced to reorganize on a national basis. The Anglican Communion in Japan asked its American and British bishops to resign. Six other of the largest denominations came together to form a national church of Japan. And all was under pressure from without, pressure which came with the putting into effect of the Religious Bodies Law of 1939.[1] This pressure is not directly related to the State cult, but is one index of the increasing regimentation which Christians must expect. And another direction in which there is less and less room for exceptions to the national uniformity is at the shrines. In both these respects Christians for the most part have found submission possible so far. Will it continue to be so, or, as was the case in the Roman Empire of Origen's time, is something else ahead?

This is enough to show that there is room for a comparison. In the light of such comparison let us examine first the renewal of the State, and the part played by the revived State religion.

Someone whose racy style has since become well

[1] *New York Sun,* October 20, 1940: *Japan Christian Quarterly,* XV, 315-326.

known has described the Japanese Renaissance at
the end of the Tokugawa Shogunate in 1868 as 'the
synthetic manufacture of a Great Power'.[1] Old Japan
had added to her nucleus of native culture all those
influences which had been wafted over from the great
civilization of the mainland, China. New Japan was
to adopt Western ways. This meant not only rail-
ways and dockyards, foreign-style buildings and frock
coats. It meant centralized government instead of
feudalism, national sentiment instead of clan loyalties,
and beyond all this a programme of imperialist expansion—instead of previous self-centredness—which
was to make Japan a Power. How was it to be done?

All the world knows how young Japanese were
selected and sent abroad. Britain was her example
in naval affairs, for a modern code of law, for a
parliamentary system. She looked to Germany for
an army, modern medicine, and a written constitution. To France and to the United States she
looked for other aspects of the new life upon which
she was entering. In every case she chose that
country where she believed the best of its kind was
to be found, and adapted that best to fit her own
need. But there remained one other question: the
spirit behind it all, the *sanction* of the new society—
where was that to be found? The first attempt to
provide a State religion capable of affording such a
sanction was by combining Buddhism and the old
indigenous Nature worship of Japan which is called
Shinto. The official aim was set down as to inspire
'reverence for the gods and love of country . . .

[1] Stephen King-Hall, *Western Civilization and the Far East,*
p. 56.

the truth of Heaven and the way of humanity . . .
respect for the Emperor and obedience to his will '.[1]
Special attention should be given to the second half
of each of these three clauses. It is this which later
becomes detached.

In the year 1875 this composite religion was
scrapped. There followed in 1882 the separation of
Sect Shinto from Shrine Shinto. The first is counted
a religion of Japan, along with Buddhism and
Christianity, and, like them, comes under the care of
the Government Department of Education (Bureau of
Religion). The second is officially explained as an
effort to maintain traditional national ritual as contributing to the national spirit. It comes under the
Home Office (Bureau of Shrines).[2] This residuum of
a religion—many Japanese would say that what
remained is not a religion at all—is the State
cultus.

In Rome, too, religion was sought as a sanction,
to provide spirit for that body which had been
formed by the unification of all the Mediterranean
world under the rule of one city-state. Ancient
society did not know a bond of union other than
the religious: the sanction behind family life was
to be found in the worship of ancestors; that behind
the city-state in the worship of its tutelary gods.
Rome as an Empire, an achievement of unity on a
new scale, demanded a new religion at its back.

' Half with conscious aim, half driven on unconsciously
by the tide of circumstances, the new empire set about

---

[1] Quoted from regulations of 1872 by D. C. Holtom, *The
National Faith of Japan*, p. 60.
[2] Holtom, p. 68.

creating a new religion. It showed extraordinary skill in constructing the new system out of the old.[1]

Those words might equally well have been written to describe Roman Emperor worship *or* Japanese Shrine Shinto.

In 1911 instructions were issued by the Minister of Education that on the occasion of festivals at the local shrine, neighbouring schools were to attend, ' to give expression to the true spirit of reverence . . . most important in establishing the foundations of national morality '. For some time enforcement or neglect of this instruction depended upon the attitude of local authorities. Not unnaturally watch was most strict where there were large non-assimilated sections of the population, i.e., in Formosa, Korea, and now in the puppet State of Manchu-kuo.[2]

The objects of reverence in the various shrines are as follows : Imperial ancestors of distinction—many of whom are legendary figures; emperors whose subjects in their lifetime rebelled; princes who for military exploits count as national heroes; subjects of exceptional patriotism; Nature-gods of old Shinto, who are counted as being imperial ancestors too, chief of these being Amaterasu-Omikami in the Grand Imperial Shrine at Ise. The purpose of these shrines is clearly stated to be to heighten national sentiment through reverence for the imperial house.

The Emperor, and reverence for him as a symbol

---

[1] W. M. Ramsay, *The Church in the Roman Empire*, p. 191.
[2] Here the shrines are ' Confucian ', but one to the Sun-Goddess was dedicated after the Manchu ' Emperor ' returned from Japan in 1940. The State cultus of the puppet must needs become that of the Empire which pulls the strings.

of the State, were similarly central in Roman State religion. In some parts of the Empire he was represented as an earthly manifestation of the god which was locally venerated. In Asia Minor an imperial cultus was set up with its own temples and priesthood, from 29 B.C. onwards. As if to explain —perhaps to excuse—the presence of the Emperor there, a shadowy being, Dea Roma, the spirit of Rome, was coupled with him as an object of worship. The State priesthood also served to supervise and control priesthoods of other religions in the locality. In Rome itself there was naturally a different approach—or rather a variety of different approaches: The divine ancestry of the Julian house was emphasized in one of the new temples set up by Augustus, to Venus Genetrix.[1] More important as an influence upon future attitudes was his setting up of the *genius* of the Emperor as central in the street shrines (*lares compitales*) throughout the city. Dead Emperors were afforded divine honours by vote of the Senate, a proceeding which seems to us a strange commentary upon the meaning of divinity! However, Japan's list to-day, as seen in those former Emperors who are represented in the shrines, is similarly selective.

Holtom points out that we have here the 'extraordinary spectacle' of a modern State trying to strengthen its hold on politics and society by use of a nature myth which belongs to the childhood of the race. The myth is that of the imperial family's descent from the Sun-Goddess, herself the daughter of the Sky-Father and Earth-Mother. 'The Emperor

[1] G. F. Moore, *History of Religion*, I, 569.

is sacred and inviolable,' says Article III of the
Japanese Constitution. 'The sacred throne, transmitted through an unbroken line . . . is immutable
as the Heavens and the Earth,' says Prince Ito in
commentary upon it. School texts base the national
history upon this myth, and make it central in
civics: 'We look up to the Emperor,' says one of the
national readers, 'even as to God.'

Perhaps one might say that if in Britain we left
the various denominations of the Christian Church
untouched, but selected from among them that
reversion to primitive tribal conceptions of the Deity,
known as British Israelitism, and made that the
State religion, we should be near the mark. To complete the nightmare one would have to imagine
Westminster Abbey, St. Paul's, and other historic
churches throughout the country separated for this
use, with compulsory pilgrimages to them on Empire
Day, Armistice Day, the King's Birthday, and so
forth. Moreover, this fantasy would be foisted upon
India, and upon the colonies, even though they not
only had no interest in the British race as the
Peculiar People, but had no connexion with any
form of that religion by misuse of whose mythology
the doctrine was being propagated.[1]

All this may sound so 'extraordinary' as to be
without parallel in history. But the *genius* explanation offered in Rome, in an attempt to rationalize
the veneration of the Emperor as something less
foreign to Roman ways than simple deification,
was essentially similar. It too was a bit of animism

[1] Compare King-Hall's analogy, connecting Adam and Eve by
genealogical tree to the Royal Family, op. cit., 287.

descended from the childhood of the race—the guardian spirit which follows a man as closely as his shadow.

Japan's enforcement of attendance at shrine worship was, we saw, most zealous on the circumference of her Empire. Rome's first compulsion was to be found in her Eastern provinces. Shrines to the Emperor here in Britain bring the thing nearer home. Tacitus tells us that one was set up at Colchester, 'that the citadel of Rome's overlordship may be beheld of men'.[1] Even so, modern Japanese would give a political rather than a religious explanation to the extension of their shrines to Formosa, Korea, Manchu-kuo—'that the New Order in East Asia may be beheld of men'.

Such is the part played by the State religion in the renewal of the State, and in the new imperialism which is its expression.

Without considering rights and wrongs, let us review facts concerning the relations of Christians with these State systems, in Rome then, and in Japan now: First I would ask you to note Acts xix. 31:

'And certain of the Asiarchs (R.V. margin) being his friends, besought him not to adventure himself into the theatre.'

These are none other than high priests of Caesar worship, *friends* of St. Paul! Their attitude shows nothing but concern for his safety, no intolerance, no idea yet of any rivalry, clash of loyalties, crisis of choice. Indeed, one would suspect, there was among them no particular enthusiasm for the worship of

[1] *Annals*, XIV, xxxi, 6.

the Emperor as a religion. Evidently St. Paul found it possible to be on good terms with them as Roman citizens like himself, members of the same educated class. The opposition which had arisen at Ephesus was neither religious nor political, but rather commercial. Its leaders were not priests, nor Asiarchs, but tradesmen—silversmiths. But, remembering this incident as an instance of the Apostle's broadmindedness, we must also recall that Christians were not yet being compelled to go to the imperial shrines. They were still sheltered under the benefit of Jewish privilege.

The reign of the Emperor Domitian, 81-96, is marked by growing attention to the national cultus. (After his death, that which the senate voted him was not *consecratio* but *damnatio*!) 'Dominus et deus noster' was how he loved to be hailed. He tried to claim for his person what others had been content to assert of their *genius*, to lay hold now on that which others hoped for at death. This is a generation later than Demetrius the silversmith. To see the changes which it brought to the Church in the city of Ephesus, one must turn to the Book of the Revelation xvii. 5, 6. How distant seem the days when the Apostle fraternized with the high priests of Caesar worship! Rome is now

'Babylon the Great, the Mother of the harlots and of the abominations of the earth . . . drunken with the blood of the saints and with the blood of the martyrs of Jesus.'

Yet Rome was never guilty of *religious* intolerance, and a Roman citizen might well have been amazed

G

at such a charge. In the words of a legal expert:

'Where religion is incorporated into politics, any re-
bellion against the established gods is apt to be regarded
as equivalent to treason against the established order of
government.'[1]

With regard to Rome, Ramsay well describes the
situation:

'Refusal to comply with the prescribed forms of
respect to the Emperor was a refusal to be a member of
the Roman unity and constituted disloyalty and treason.
. . . Pliny found the procedure already established that
a charge of Christianity should be tested by calling on the
accused to perform the ceremonies of loyal service and
worship to the Emperor.'[2]

Religious intolerance is equally disclaimed by modern
Japan. Says an exponent of Shrine Shinto:

'In the case of a civilized country there must exist
freedom of faith. . . . Yet for a Japanese subject to
refuse to honour the ancestors of the Emperor is disloyal.
Indeed a Japanese out of his duty as subject must honour
the ancestors of the Emperor. This cannot be a matter
of choice. It is a duty. Therefore this cannot be regarded as a religion.'[3]

Except for that last sentence, the passage could be
re-written with 'Roman' instead of 'Japanese' and
its reference pushed back to the second century
instead of the twentieth. There is the same anti-
thesis, religious toleration as an accepted State policy

[1] Sir Frederick Pollock, *Essays in Jurisprudence and Ethics*,
pp. 147f.
[2] *The Church in the Roman Empire*, p. 275.
[3] Quoted by Holtom, op. cit., p. 69.

on the one hand, and required submission to a State cultus on the other. Christians are faced with the same dilemma: they are not disloyal to the State, but if, from religious motives, they reject the State cultus, they will be regarded and treated as disloyal. The way out of the dilemma appears to be different. In the Roman Empire, Christians said, 'Then we must be misunderstood,' and endured the punishment of traitors. In the Japanese Empire, the Government is saying, 'Therefore this cannot be regarded as a religion.' That is the difference. Does such assurance on the part of the State make all the difference?

This compulsion, which we have noted at the end of the first and beginning of the second centuries, did not continue as the invariable rule. In Japan attempts have been made to separate expressions of loyalty from that obeisance which had associations with pagan worship: Christians were to be allowed to bow to the flag, not to the shrine; or Christians at the shrine were to be allowed to pray to their own God on behalf of the Emperor, while disregarding his ancestors. Something entirely similar happened in the second century. Christians were sometimes allowed by a sympathetic official to take the oath *per salutem Imperatoris*, which they felt they could do with a clear conscience, instead of *per genium Caesaris*, which had associations with the heathen pantheon and was therefore refused.[1] A friendly authority might accept this oath as a sufficient test of loyalty. For that was still, indeed more than ever, the State's concern.

[1] Tertullian, *Apology*, 32.

' Pagans were becoming increasingly anxious at the
progress of a belief which seemed to destroy the loyalty
of the masses to tradition, and therewith their loyalty to
the State itself.'[1]

But an official less friendly would be more exacting
in his requirements, and that meant martyrdom.
With the coming of the great State-sponsored persecutions in the latter half of the third century, there
would be less room for such clemency. Then the
Empire's motive was to force a crisis—and where it
could, to force apostasy.

In Japan, these attempts at compromise have
already been disallowed. The act must be one of
obeisance towards the Kami[2] of the shrine. The
only room for compromise is in the matter of mental
reservations. The State, so far from requiring any
declaration of faith concerning the obeisance or its
objects, discourages any discussion. The easiest way is
to say, ' This is not religion,' and submit. This way
is recommended, nay, urged, by the State. Again I
remind you, *that* is the difference—it almost seems
the only difference—in the position of Christians in
the two Empires.

Finally, let us apply the light of history to some
current statements about the situation in Japan.
Several reasons have been advanced why Christians
ought to be able—as indeed most Japanese seem to
have been able so far—to submit to the requirements
of the State. By some it is said that ' the idol is
nothing ':

---

[1] Hugh Last in *Journal of Roman Studies*, XXVII, Pt. i, 1937.
[2] Difficult to translate into English; ' numina ' seems to fit best.

'There is no suggestion of idolatry because the Christian knows in his heart that an idol is nothing. Therefore if he asserts that his bow is one of secular deference to national authority, no harm is involved in obeisance at the shrines.'[1]

The best comment upon this kind of casuistry is Tertullian's:

'We cannot be held to do harm to (by refusing to worship) that which has no existence. . . . Some indeed think it a piece of insanity that, when it is in our power to offer sacrifice at once and go away unharmed, holding as ever our convictions, yet we prefer an obstinate persistence in our confession instead of safety. You advise us, forsooth, to take an unjust advantage of you. But we know . . . who is at the bottom of it all.'[2]

He means the devil.

Others argue that the founders of State Shinto were themselves irreligious, therefore that which they founded cannot rightly be regarded as religion:

'Japanese Christians know that the men of the Meiji Restoration (of 1868) who devised the cult of national Shinto and incorporated these practices into the educational system . . . were self-confessed agnostics and nationalists. This seems to be true of many present-day officials who require the observance of these practices. This makes it easier to accept. . . .'[3]

Of course it is possible that the martyrs of the Western Church in its heroic period were mistaken. But to them too was open exactly the same escape:

[1] *International Review of Missions*, April 1940, p. 168.
[2] *Apology*, 26.
[3] *International Review of Missions*, April 1940, p. 181.

' Hadrian himself was quite alive to the fact that the State religion was a sham, and, looked at as a religion, a failure; but he knew also that it was the keystone of the Imperial policy.'[1]

So wrote Professor Ramsay in the distant days of 1895. He little realized that during his lifetime at the other side of the world a march of events had begun which was to make these careful judgments of history applicable to a living situation.

Others again have said that refusal would be a falsification of the facts:

' Christian leaders . . . see the difficulties that would be involved in a refusal to observe these practices which are regarded as expressions of loyalty and patriotism. Japanese Christians are loyal. . . . To refuse . . . would be to brand themselves with a false label. It would also be an invitation to the authorities to put a ban on the entire Christian movement.'[2]

Strange things happen in Japan. A Christian youth seeking admission to a State university was asked at his interview, ' Who is the greater, your God, or the Emperor? ' With such an attitude abroad, it is falsification of facts in the other direction which we as Christians should watch. To sum up:

' As the Tambaram findings say, the question at what point the challenge is to be resisted " must ultimately be left to the judgment and conscience of the church most

[1] *The Church in the Roman Empire*, p. 324.
[2] *International Review of Missions*, April 1940, p. 181.

concerned ".   That judgment will not be sound if it is
ignorant of light and leading which have shone through
dark periods before, nor will that conscience be fully
Christian if it is forgetful of the great cloud of witnesses.'[1]

[1] A sentiment I expressed in *The Life of the Church*, Tambaram Madras Series, Vol. IV, p. 262.

CHAPTER VI

THE UNIVERSAL CHURCH AND ITS LOCAL MANIFESTATION

ONE of the most difficult sections of the Madras Conference was that which had to deal with the relation of Christianity to other faiths. The discussion there begun is admirably continued—by eight scholars of eight different nationalities!—in *The Authority of Faith.*[1] I can best introduce you to the problem by smuggling you in to listen to the actual discussions at Madras. We shall choose a moment when representatives of each extreme are speaking.

The first is an Indian: ' Jesus Christ comes not to destroy but to fulfil. Even so He comes to India, not to pull down the old spiritual home. Rather His demand is the making of a new window where before there was a blank wall, or the replacing of smoky oil lamps by electric light.' I do not know how that strikes you. I am wondering, with a shudder, if he is going on to say ' h. and c. in every room '. The building analogy is an unfortunate choice. New Testament passages leap to one's mind about the One Foundation—not a new window—and the Chief Corner-Stone—not mere electric wiring. And so we ask ourselves, Is this enough?

[1] Tambaram Madras Series, Vol. I.

Next a German: ' There is no such thing as what
we used to call the Comparative Study of Religions.
You cannot compare because there is no common
standard. Christ is not fulfilment of but judgment upon
our religious past. Even the Hebrew of the Hebrews,
heir to the fullest apprehension of God yet to be found
among men, had to say, " What things were gain to
me, these have I counted loss for Christ." '   Again
I am uneasy, this time because of the *unrelatedness*
of pre-Christian and Christian experiences. St. Paul
spoke other words: ' He left not Himself without
witness. . . . As certain even of your own poets have
said. . . . What therefore ye worship in ignorance,
this set I forth unto you.' Is not this an overstate-
ment?

National sentiment, especially where it is of recent
growth, makes some unduly sensitive of seeming
criticism upon their cultural heritage. Others speak
as though the whole of Christian truth can be summed
up in terms of one rediscovered theological emphasis.
The Conference had to declare, ' Christians are not
agreed. This is a matter urgently demanding thought
and united study.'[1] Perhaps the mistake is to imagine
that by further thought and study we should arrive
at an ' either . . . or ' solution. The glory of our
Lord is that with Him may be found room for ' both
. . . and . . .' He is fulfilment, not in the sense of
adding a bit more to that which was almost complete
without Him, but as ' faith is the *hypostasis* of things
hoped for ',[2] as a real presence may fulfil the dim
perceptions of a dream. He is judgment upon our
past, even our religious past at its best, since He not

[1] *The Authority of the Faith*, p. 211.   [2] Hebrews xi. 1.

only satisfies the desires of every living thing, but awakens new, undreamed-of, desires for things higher, deeper, eternal.

The practical part of the problem is how to relate Christianity to the background of pre-Christian thought so that it will remain Christianity, but cease to be a foreign faith. This is, of course, a great historic problem, one which belongs to the second century of the Church's life. Let us remind ourselves once again that in the lands of the Younger Churches it is the second century which is upon us now.

In the earliest extant letter of St. Paul there occurs a sentence which may be taken as ' convenient summary of the earliest Pauline teaching . . . the most effective means of reaching the consciences and satisfying the religious instincts of their heathen auditors '.[1]

' Ye turned to God from idols, to serve a living and true God, and to wait for his Son from heaven, whom he raised from the dead, even Jesus, who delivers us from the wrath to come.'[2]

If it is a summary of missionary preaching, it is also a summary of the great articles of belief among those who had been won over from paganism:[3] (1) Monotheism, (2) Second Advent, (3) Resurrection, (4) A Saviour from Judgment. Notice that such a statement of the faith bears two marks. It is essentially primitive and essentially Jewish. I say primitive, because it belongs to the days when the striking turn-

[1] G. Milligan, *St. Paul's Epistles to the Thessalonians*, pp. xlii f.
[2] 1 Thessalonians i. 9, 10.
[3] F. C. Burkitt, *Church and Gnosis*, pp. 10ff., to which I am largely indebted in working out this view of Gnosticism.

over has been made—from idols to God, from the
many to the One, from the dead to the Living, from
the false to the True. Ask to-day any first generation
Christian in China what it means to be a Christian
and he will answer unhesitatingly, 'Pu pai p'u-sa'
('We don't worship idols').[1] That may seem to you
a disappointingly negative description. But mistake
him not: the reason is the same—this tremendous
choice is the experience which overshadows all else.
The second mark (items 2, 3, 4, above) is the imprint
of the missionary. Here in Thessalonians the statement of the faith for Greek Christians is essentially
Jewish. 'We preach not ourselves,' says the Apostle
to the Gentiles. But we can preach the truth only as
we see it; we can see it only from our own stand-
point, and describe it only in our own terms. Even
so the faith of the first generation Christian to-day,
apart from this primary and overwhelming experience
of choice, is in terms learned from the missionary,
translated from a foreign environment. Ask that
Chinese Christian to go on and tell you more, and
from his answer you may guess to which European
or American mission he belongs.

St. Paul was the hero of the Church's first crisis,
the conflict with the Judaisers. Christianity was not
to be a sect within the national religion, but the
faith which would claim mankind. He thus became
the pioneer of all pioneer missionaries. There is one
question however, which, while it ought to belong to
the mind of the pioneer—and it was in the mind of
St. Paul—can never be his battle. The pioneer re-
discovers, or demonstrates anew, the universality of

[1] See my *Chinese Church in Action*, p. 57.

the faith, but he is doomed to preach it in terms of
foreign thought. Only later can it become indigenous.
Care over that becoming he must leave to his successors. In the findings of the Madras Conference,
it is stated:

'We strongly affirm that the Gospel should be expressed in indigenous forms, and that in methods of
worship, institutions, architecture, etc., the spiritual heritage of the nation . . . should be taken into use. . . .
The endeavour to give Christ His rightful place in the
heart of a people who have not known Him—so that He
will neither be a foreigner, nor will be distorted by pre-
Christian patterns of thought—is a great and exacting
spiritual task in the fulfilling of which a young church
can bring a rich contribution of her own to the Church
Universal.'[1]

This 'great and exacting spiritual task' belongs to
the age after the great pioneers, the post-apostolic
age, the second century of the missionary movement—*us*.

By the second century there are many reasons
why expression of the faith must change. 'Ye
turned. . . .' No, they did not—they were born of
Christian parents. To that one overshadowing experience of choice they are strangers. Strangers too
to those alien apostles. The Jewish missionaries are
long since gone. Jerusalem itself as the mother-church
is gone. The great figures of Christian history at the
turn of the century—Ignatius, Clement, Polycarp,
Justin, Aristides—are not Jews. The day of indigenous leadership has come. Neither the simplicity nor

[1] *The World Mission of the Church*, p. 53; *The Authority of
the Faith*, pp. 213f.

the borrowed nature of the primitive statement can satisfy. They must have a faith which is related to the culture around them.

So comes the second great crisis. The first was bound up with the origin of the missionary movement. The second is the problem of Christianity's indigenous expression.[1] 'Leave us free to make our own heresies,' said a young Ceylonese minister at Madras. I do not know how seriously he meant it. Heresy-hunting has fallen into disfavour in this age of broad toleration. We must ever beware lest our progress in broad-mindedness should reach the infinite breadth of vacuity. Still there is something to be said for this attitude in the churches of the West. If this is not a heresy-hunting, neither is it a heresy-making age. But heresy is an ever-present danger to the Younger Churches. *It ought to be.* They are precisely at that period of development.

That which was wrong with Gnosticism, in seeking to attain this desirable end of indigenous expression, was that it led not to a reinterpretation but to a ruin. The work of the Gnostics was not to bring essential Christianity to clear and vigorous expression through the use of indigenous symbols. It was to recast Christianity in the mould of indigenous philosophy. What came out was shaped by the mould. That which had been decisive was a pre-Christian apprehension of life. Something of Christianity was left adhering to the surface—that was all.

The thought-environment of Indian Christians

---

[1] See H. Kraemer, *The Christian Message in a Non-Christian World*, especially pp. 307-335; G. E. Phillips, *The Gospel in the World*, ch. xiv.

is syncretism, of Chinese Christians humanism, of Japanese Christians nationalism; African Christians are obsessed by problems arising from a polygamous society. Thus each is tempted to forsake one part of the Christian·tradition : the Indian, Christian history; the Chinese, Christian theology; the Japanese, Christian universality; the African, Christian morality. These are not meant to be sweeping generalizations but rather typical examples. Indian thinkers are tempted to let go of history, to identify Christian experience with Hindu mystical communion with the Soul-of-the-world, to apologize for any special mention of Jesus of Nazareth.[1] Chinese thinkers are tempted to let go theology : it does not matter what you believe about our Lord's relation to the Godhead, if you accept Him as Ideal Man, One with a higher ethic than the *Chun Tzu* (Princely Man) of Confucius.[2] Japanese Christians in September 1939 resolved to ' co-operate in the realization ' of the New Order in East Asia, and to ' stress the harmony between Christianity and the national objectives '.[3] A year later most of the churches had submitted to Government pressure for reorganization on a national basis.[4] Much unrest in African churches is due to

[1] See *Rethinking Christianity in India* for a weakening of the position of the historic Christ (e.g. pp. 75f.); distaste for our historic connexion with the Old Testament; disowning of the historic Church. Much of it might have come from the pen of Marcion.

[2] Professor T. C. Chao in an article, ' The Future of the Church ', says that the ' naturalism and humanism ' of his environment, with the ' shallowness ' of his own religious experience, ' can at best lead the Chinese Christian to an adoption of the ethical teachings of Jesus. . . . Confucianist under a different name.'

[3] *National Christian Council of Japan Bulletin.*

[4] See p. 90 above.

what is sometimes regarded as the finnickiness of missionary-imported traditions with regard to sex. It is all the modern equivalent of ancient Gnosticism. It is our second-century crisis, demanding our continued brotherly help and sympathy and prayer. Yes, *elder*-brotherly, for it is upon us that they depend for that experience which is history. A sense of history is the outstanding need of the Younger Churches. As the Madras findings say,[1] one of the chief tasks of the modern missionary is 'to embody and transmit the experience of the Universal Church.' That is no small order. It demands our utmost respect, both for the task itself, and for the men who go to it.

I always find it easier to think of the relation of Christianity to the non-Christian religions, when the terms of reference point me, not to a disembodied Christianity, but to the Christian Church. It is here that one can see plainly that the ' both . . . and . . .' solution must be the right one. The seed has life in itself, the same life generation after generation and whatever the field. But the seed is planted in the local soil. It is through that soil that its nourishment must come, and it must grow. Or, to change the parable, Christianity is represented by two lines, one downward, the other across. The downward one is the continuity of Christian experience, the unchangeable 'faith once for all delivered to the saints', the 'one, holy, catholic, and apostolic Church'. The line across is that which reaches out to the environment, relates it to the here, and now, our faith and our Church. Is it fanciful to think that it takes both these

[1] *The Life of the Church*, Tambaram Madras Series, Vol. IV, p. 253.

lines to form the symbol of our faith, the Cross? Let us look at each in turn.

First, the local manifestation: I have lived in China, wandered in the Philippines and Japan, and now most recently have visited India. In all these lands, I fear, we have transplanted the traditional architecture of our own worst period. We have scattered Asia with mock-Gothic and other Victorian ugliness. And in most we have acted as though the nurture of Christ's flock were inseparable from the bleating of American organs—instead of using the simple instruments of the place and consecrating their own music from the start.

But do not put down all such mistakes to the stupidity of the missionary. Often one is faced with the opposition of the people themselves. While any of the 'turned-to-God-from-idols' attitude remains, that which is foreign will be welcomed because it is foreign. I recall a new church in one Chinese city. The (missionary) architect was keen on Chinese styles. He had given us a splendid pagoda instead of a steeple —a pagoda surmounted by a great cross. The building committee, composed of responsible Chinese business men, was considering the furnishings. I ventured to write urging that they should get a Chinese bell. Anyone who has heard the boom echo and re-echo over the hills, as a monk in the neighbouring monastery has struck regular beats with his wooden ram, will agree that in China are cast some of the best bells in the world. They considered my proposition—and they bought a bell from Woolwich. They said, 'We want nothing in God's house which will remind us whence we have come.' One's use of the indigenous must always be conditioned by the conscience of one's people. Sometimes it means a long wait.

But there have been some amazing triumphs of grace in this regard. I was charmed by the Telegu lyrics which I heard in South Indian churches, sung to strange one-string fiddles, flutes, tambourines, and cymbals. I thought sadly of the popular hymn in China which still tends to be Sankey on the harmonium. I quote from my Indian travel diary:

We saw dancing in the courtyard of the church. The religious dance is something carried over from pre-Christian days. The leader tells a Bible story, e.g. the deliverance from Egypt. The dancers form two concentric circles, moving in opposite directions. Each dancer has a stick, and as he passes each member of the other ring he taps his stick. Feet beat rhythmically, sticks tap to the same rhythm, and through it all come the chanted words of the story, with a refrain (like ' The Lord came down to Egypt '), oft repeated, in which all the dancers join. The story advances very slowly and in something like House-that-Jack-built method. Needless to say this is a great means of teaching Bible knowledge. On summer nights they will go on with one story, elaborating it by description of what everyone wore, and how everyone felt, into the small hours. Whereas if one told a straight story the non-Christian neighbour would be unmoved, and the Christian himself might not remember it.

Here you have something from pre-Christian life taken up and baptized into the Christian religion by the first missionaries, in a way which was not attempted in Northern Europe till centuries after its

H

conversion.[1] Indeed the adoption of the ring dance and the round into the Christian carol never won the Church's official approval. What Dr. Coulton calls ' Medieval Puritanism ' continued to frown upon the dance.[2] If in Europe it was given a tardy baptism, it never grew up and came to confirmation. The medieval missionaries thought that the pagan dances which they found in England—of which ' Ring a ring o' Roses ' and ' Here we go round the mulberry bush ' are lineal descendants—were of the devil. They were at that time hardly so innocent as these childish games have become! They were connected with nature worship, and, being originally meant to excite the fertility spirits to do their work, often excited the dancers to indulge their own passions. The Church tried to suppress them, but it did not succeed.

It was left to the Franciscans, who in so many ways brought religion nearer to the life of the countryside than it ever had been, to attempt to claim this custom for the service of the Church. Just as in my South India church courtyard, they let the people dance to Christian themes on English village greens before the parish church. They made a circle while the leader sang, joined hands to dance around him, came in with the recurring ' burden ' of the story as he unfolded it. It was a late attempt, coming to its own in the fifteenth century, and then apparently dying away. There are tendencies to idealize the medieval Church at the expense of the modern— especially of the Protestant. When we criticize our

[1] H. Maynard Smith, *Pre-Reformation England*, pp. 155ff.
[2] *Five Centuries of Religion*, I, 531-538.

nineteenth-century predecessors, let us recall that as missionaries they were in this respect centuries ahead of what might have been expected of them.

But with regard to what I have called the local manifestation, there was some extraordinary broad-mindedness when the Church was first established among our heathen ancestors. Pope Gregory the Great had already shown it in his instructions to Augustine not to feel himself bound in any slavish spirit to every detail of the Roman rite:

'If you have found anything either in the Roman, Gallican, or any other church, which may be more acceptable to almighty God, carefully make choice of the same, and sedulously teach the church of the English, which as yet is new in the faith, whatsoever you can gather from the several churches. For things are not to be loved for the sake of places, but places for the sake of good things.'[1]

A model of missionary statesmanship is his letter to the Abbot Mellitus whom he sent in the year 601 with reinforcements for the mission:[2] If soundly built, temples are not to be destroyed but cleansed and consecrated, that people may 'more freely resort to the places to which they have been accustomed'. Local usage is to be adopted and baptized, even the 'slaughter of many oxen' for sacrificial feasts; but now the feasting shall be in honour of God and the saints, not of demons. 'He who tries to mount to the highest place must go up by steps and not by leaps.' Gregory even advances in support of this practice the theory that the sacrificial system of

---

[1] Bede, *Ecclesiastical History*, I, xxvii.
[2] *Epistles*, xi, 76.

Egypt may have influenced the Mosaic ritual. How modern (you may say, how like the author of this book) he sounds, both in his concern for the 'indigenous' and in his search for parallel situations in earlier Church History! We know that something like this procedure does lie behind the foundation even of our most famous churches. The mother-church of English Christianity at Canterbury rose from a ruin already old 'built by the ancient workmanship of Roman Christians'.[1] Some old churches were not in ruins but had been desecrated by pagan worship since the Anglo-Saxon invasion.[2] These were restored under a general licence from King Ethelbert, and reconsecrated by the Archbishop. Later tradition speaks of the paganism which was supplanted as being that of the great gods of Greece and Rome. Thus Stow, speaking of the discovery near St. Paul's in 1316 of 'bones. of oxen and kine', says that this

'confirms. greatly the opinion of those which have reported that of old times there had been a temple of Jupiter, and that there was daily a sacrifice of beasts.'[3]

One might more reasonably be reminded of Pope Gregory's letter about the 'slaughter of many oxen' in English pagan feasts. A charter of Westminster Abbey, which is still in the chapter-house and is ascribed to King Offa (758-796), speaks of the place of its foundation as 'loco terrabili'—'a dreadful place', being quotation of the Vulgate, Genesis xxviii. 17.[4] Later tradition speaks of a ruined temple to Apollo

---

[1] Bede, Ecclesiastical History, I, xxxiii.
[2] Bright, Early English Church History, pp. 61f.
[3] Quoted by G. E. B. in Cathedrals, p. 8.
[4] Bright, op. cit., pp. 101f.

on the site. Roman or English, the reference to a
theophany may well imply pre-Christian religious
associations.

But if you are surprised at such enlightened toler-
ance in a bishop of Rome over thirteen centuries ago,
it is nothing to my amazement at our mid-nineteenth
century missionary predecessors. Remember the attitude among pious evangelicals towards dancing then.
Yet when the call of God had summoned them from
their narrow Victorian environment and set them
down in an Indian jungle, they were able to take
hold of a religious dance and consecrate it to the
service of the Church. Can you explain it apart from
the grace of God?

Though the use of indigenous music and original
hymns is of later development in China, there you
will find other parts of the ' local manifestation ' long
and well established. Chinese Christians have one
festival which is not on our calendar. In the Spring,
the males of non-Christian families go out to the
family graves. They add more sods to each mound,
crowning them all with red paper. They fire crackers
to scare away evil influences. They burn ' spirit
money ' as offerings to the needs of the dead. Christians still keep the Spring festival. They go out men
and women together, for in Christ ' there can be no
male and female '.[1] They go not by families but in
a body, one household of the faith. They sing glad
hymns to One who has vanquished death. In prayer
they are joined to all the companies of heaven. The
festival has become fully Christian.

The story is told of an up-country Chinese

[1] Galatians iii. 28.

merchant who advised an English business acquaintance to try to get hold of a book he had been reading.
' I don't know whether there is an English translation
yet. Its name is *New Testament.*' Apocryphal or
not, there is this amount of truth in it: parts of the
New Testament are better understood in Chinese
than in English. In a Chinese family there is a
different word for ' brother ' when applied to the
eldest boy. According to Confucian ethical tradition
he has quite a different station. He does really share
the parental authority. There is an especially close
' father-firstborn ' relationship. There is a ready
understanding of the Only-begotten from the Father,
who is at the same time the Firstborn of many
brethren. In Taoist philosophic thought the *Tao*
(Way) has been all but personified—a metaphysical
principle which precedes all being (' Silent, ineffable,
abiding alone and changing not'[1]), and from which
all being proceeds (' Mother of all things . . . loving,
nourishing, and ruling all things '). With as much
understanding as those who first read the beginning
of the Fourth Gospel in Greek, Chinese can read:

' In the beginning was the *Tao*, and the *Tao* was with
God, and the *Tao* was God. . . . and the *Tao* became
flesh and dwelt among us. . . .'

There are theological terms of Chinese Buddhism
which Christians in China twelve hundred years ago
were already successfully borrowing[2]—just as Western
Fathers evolved expressions of their faith in terms of
Greek philosophy. Very like the three *hypostaseis*
of Neo-Platonism, οὐσία (Primal Being), νοῦς (Mind),

[1] *Tao-teh-Ching*, the classic of Taoism.
[2] My *Church of the T'ang Dynasty*, pp. 107ff.

ψυχή (Soul), there are the three aspects of the *Chen-ju* (True Norm) of Mahayana philosophy: *t'i* (God in Himself), *hsiang* (God as revealed in His effulgence), *yung* (God as active energy in His creation). Perhaps we of the modern age have been less daring than those Nestorians who first brought the faith. Much of the adventure of making a Chinese theology awaits the Young Church's fuller development. But from these illustrations you can already see, as in one of the better-known examples of Chinese Christian art, the Three Religions of China, like the Magi, bowing before the young Child.

Have you ever thought that the Church will not have become truly catholic until wise men of every land have opened their treasures and offered to Him their gifts? While one of the 'local manifestations' is lacking or undeveloped, the Universal Church itself is incomplete.[1]

It is important to remember, whether your work is in Perth or in Peking, in Tottenham or in Timbuctoo, that that which you serve is the Universal Church, nothing less. How little the ordinary church-goer has realized it was illustrated when someone asked, 'Why should we take our religion to the Far East?' I said, 'How long has Christianity been ours?' For answer I turned up another letter written by Pope Gregory the Great to the Patriarch of Alexandria in the year 597.[2] You will remember that according

[1] For further illustration of the use of indigenous forms, see H. P. Thompson, *Worship in Other Lands*; M. H. Harper in *Environmental Factors in Christian History*, pp. 339-344 (India); Mabel Shaw, *God's Candlelights* (Rhodesia); D. J. Fleming, *Each with His Own Brush* (Christian Art), *Heritage of Beauty* (Architecture), *Christian Symbols in a World Community*.
[2] *Epistles*, viii, 30.

to Bede's story of the fair-headed slave boys ('Not Angles but Angels'), Gregory could not resist a pun. This letter is further evidence:

'The nation of the Angles, *set in an angle of the world,* remained until now believing in the worship of stocks and stones.'

He goes on to tell of the 'happy success' of Augustine's mission. It is not only that he wants to pun. That is how he regards these barbarian kingdoms. So far from our being central in Christendom, he calls us 'the end of the world'. The Church was planted in northern England thirty-eight years later, when Bishop Aidan came from the island of Iona to Holy Isle, off the Northumbrian coast. The year 635 is a year to remember. It marks the beginning of the permanent triumph of the faith in this our land. And that same year another bishop, the Persian Alopen, having crossed the highest mountains in the world and some of its most dreadful deserts, arrived at the capital of the greatest civilization upon earth —China.[1] Our Christianity? For Anglo-Saxons and for Chinese, Church History opens in the very same year!

The Church is not something which belonged to the West, and which, only recently, we have taken East. If we are awarded only a dead heat with the 'heathen Chinee', we are knocked out of the competition by the Indian. The Church in South India has a tradition of apostolic foundation, which even if you do not accept it as history, is so hard to dis-

[1] See my *Church of the T'ang Dynasty.*

prove that you cannot mention in the same breath our legends of Joseph of Arimathæa, the holy grail, and the flowering thorn. The Church was certainly planted in India long before our ancestors were in England at all. The Church was, is, and always will be, the *Universal* Church, attaining its local expression in this land and in that, until it shall be so in every land.

It is not only my rather ignorant questioner (above) who did not believe in foreign missions. My concern is a change of attitude in those who do. An old pillar of the Church prayed in a missionary prayer meeting, ' Lord, we thank Thee that Thine arm can reach even to China.' As though God were sitting in Britain, but had to lean far over to touch East Asia! Our attitude may never have been such with regard to the Almighty, but most of us have been brought up to think in that way of the Church.

About the year 1690 the Emperor K'ang Hsi complained to the Jesuit fathers, who were in good hope of converting him:

' If all this be true, how is it that God waits for over sixteen hundred years before giving us any knowledge of it? How is it that the Chinese are left out, and only the barbarians are mentioned? '

The answer should have been that God did not wait; that from the days of the Apostles the Church pushed eastwards; that in spite of man's delays it arrived in 635; that thenceforth, apart from one break (*c.* 1370-1550), the Church is either present in Chinese territory or pressing China-wards.

The question of K'ang Hsi is still asked. In China

during the years 1925-8, in India, Burma, Ceylon, Thailand, Japan—whenever and wherever excess of nationalist zeal breaks out, anti-Christians charge the Church with foreign-ness. Christians for the most part have nothing to answer. They themselves are only too conscious of being a late appendage to a predominantly foreign institution. This tragic failure to develop a right church-consciousness in the Younger Churches is due to the fact that we of the Older have failed to apprehend the meaning of the Universal Church.

For all of us Christian history must be presented as being primarily the progress of the Church towards the realization of its universality. Central, and giving meaning to the whole, must be that part of the progress which, in every age, brings the Church nearer towards *my land and me*.[1] Africa, India, the Far East, need to be shown more clearly each its own main line of interest; to know that the Church was never foreign, was always meant to come to them, and was always coming. Men of the modern missionary movement need to know that what they are doing is not transplanting a foreign institution, but making up for delays, failures, faithlessnesses of the past by helping now some thwarted local out-working of the Universal Church—which is the fulfilment of the eternal will of God.

This view makes all our service so much grander and more glorious—and so inevitable.

I repeat, Christianity is represented by two lines, one downward, the Universal Church; one across, the

---

[1] I have worked out this idea fairly fully in *The Life of the Church*, Tambaram Madras Series, Vol. IV, pp. 258-271.

local manifestation. And I venture now to answer what before I asked: It is *not* fanciful to think that it takes both to form the symbol of our faith, the Cross.

PART III

EDUCATION FOR WORLD-CHURCHMANSHIP

CHAPTER VII

THE WORLD-CHURCH AND RELIGIOUS EDUCATION

Is there any nation other than the British which has such a knack of doing things of immense consequence by accident, or at any rate as an unconsidered side-line? Queen Elizabeth gave a charter to a company of merchant adventurers, and later an empire fell into their lap. We went on keeping up the fiction of the East India Company, the veriest side-line of our national life, and did not recognize the existence of the Indian Empire till we had almost lost it in the mutiny of 1857.

In an entirely comparable way, as I have already shown, we have neglected to adjust ourselves to real facts with regard to the Kingdom of God.[1] Our land became the centre of the modern missionary movement. The German Pietists and Moravians were first, but we outstripped them. Now Americans may be due to take over the lead, but it has been ours through the period of greatest achievement. The year 1942 marks one century and a half since the publication of the *Enquiry into the Obligations of Christians to use Means for the Conversion of the Heathens*,[2] by the 'consecrated cobbler', as Sydney

---

[1] See pp. 61-65 above. [2] Republished in facsimile 1891.

Smith called him. 'Who was Sydney Smith?' some nowadays may ask.[1] No one needs to ask 'Who was William Carey?' Things have to that extent come out of the hole and corner in which they began. But consider: 1793, the following year, begins that positive spate of missionary societies. The nineteenth century was to continue prolific in this matter of extra-ecclesiastical societies—religious side-lines, we might say. Missionaries took the fashion with them. When they came upon a special need, these servants of the societies called for a sub-society to be formed. What marvellous names our predecessors gave them! Dickens hardly exaggerates when he describes in *Pickwick* the Reverend Mr. Stiggins' 'Society for providing the infant negroes of the West Indies with flannel waistcoats and moral pocket-handkerchiefs'. How do you like, for example, the 'Calcutta Female Juvenile Society for the Education of Native Females', founded by Hannah Marshman, wife of Carey's colleague, in 1819?

The cause of Foreign Missions still keeps the form of the side-line. Most communions carry on this work through the extra-ecclesiastical society. In a few, such as the Church of Scotland, and the Methodist Church, it is placed, as directly as Home Missions, under the control of our church courts; but when it comes to the side-line mentality, I doubt if we have room to thank God that we are not as other men. The members of our congregations, even many of our ministers, think of missionary work almost as did the absent-minded professor in the story: he consented

[1] Founder of the *Edinburgh Review* 1802, and canon of St. Paul's. See *Dictionary of National Biography*.

to take the chair at an S.P.C.K. meeting, and opened the affair with a moving speech about the prevention of cruelty to animals. Foreign Missions rank in popular esteem among the minor charities.

Compare with that the estimate of that historian who is laying us all under obligation by his great work, *A History of the Expansion of Christianity*, Professor Latourette of Yale. At the end of volume three[1] he looks forward to this modern period, and writes:

'When Waterloo brought the Napoleonic Wars to their close . . .'

(let us notice that it was during those so strangely similar years when Britain alone was untrampled by the invader, an unlikely season for any fresh movement to begin)

'. . . the new tides of life swelled to a flood. Protestant Christianity became more vigorous than ever before. The Roman Catholic Church experienced an unprecedented revival. The expansion of Europe continued at a quickened pace, and paralleling it . . . Christianity spread more rapidly and over a wider area than ever before. Upon the culture of occidental people Christianity continued to have a profound effect, in some places more pronounced than at any previous time. Among non-occidental peoples Christianity became more potent as a transformer and moulder of individuals, of groups, and of cultures, than at any time in its history. Christianity entered upon the century of its greatest influence.'

That is what the missionary movement of the last one hundred and fifty years means. It means so much

[1] p. 457.

I

that, whereas eighteen hundred years of the story have taken three volumes, Latourette estimates that he will need the same amount of space for this century and a half, the greatest period of Christian history.

To return to the comparison with which we began: long after we had, inadvertently, become an empire, we continued, as far as the outlook of our citizens was concerned, to merit the epithet, ' nation of shopkeepers '. Education for citizenship was almost unknown. In 1868 Matthew Arnold pleaded for the training of teachers with ' broad views over the history of our race . . . and its connexion which universal history gives '. But till about 1900 we were one of the most backward nations in the teaching of history. The mass of our people was little equipped to be citizens of a great empire central in the life of the world. However we had, again by accident, begun to do something to develop a ruling class, with a tradition and a training of its own. For this we must look beyond Matthew Arnold, inspector of schools, to his father, Arnold of Rugby, and to the public school tradition which he did so much to uplift. A couple of B.B.C. comedians have set the fashion of laughing at the ' old school tie '. But the empire which we won by one accident we have run by another—a type of education which just happened to fit in with our responsibilities.

When I turn to the affairs of the Kingdom of God, I feel that something of the same has happened. The greatest period of Christian history! The Church is in ideal always the same. The difference is that so much more of the ideal with regard to its universality has now been realized.[1] The Church as a matter of fact *is* more than it has ever been before. Have we a churchmanship to match the hour? Education for churchmanship—ah, where is it in these home parishes? Are we to remain in this regard a nation of shopkeepers? And what of those who receive training that they may lead and rule the Church? We cannot be content with any happy accident: we must be sure that we are giving purposefully that type of religious education to the laity, and theological education to the clergy, which will fit them for their responsibilities. Such is the relevance of re-considering, and where necessary reshaping, the whole business of training to fit this great new era of the World-wide Church. 'Education for World-Church-manship' needs to become something more than a slogan. It should be the mark of Sunday-school and Bible-class syllabuses; the subject for church fellow-ships and study groups; still more important, the guide to all preparation for confirmation and church-membership. To go back a stage further, it should become the standard against which all theological education is judged. As the way in which the ministry is educated is decisive of the minister's way in educating his people, it is by discussing chiefly theological education that I may best illustrate my meaning.

In writing about the reshaping of training I am conscious of two strong prejudices: one, that of ministers who believe themselves to have been well-trained; two, that of professors who are sceptical of all reshaping. I can sympathize. I served on the staff

[1] See pp. 34f., 39f. above.

of a theological college in China where one of my colleagues was always advocating change in educational
methods: Put it in the pot, give another stir, and see
what comes out! Generally it was some variation of
the project method: he would have all our teaching
related to the practical work of the students in small
churches in surrounding villages. I was teaching
Church History, and as things came up I was to
seize my opportunity: an evangelistic effort?—then
'Evangelism down the Ages'; a vaccination campaign?—'The Church and Public Health'. . . . I
ventured to remind him that in Church History there
was a certain time sequence that had to be considered,
and also a certain content of knowledge to be got over
against the too swift passage of time. So I have little
in the way of radical reform in mind. Theology, Old
Testament, New Testament, and Church History
will, I hope, remain the big four of theological education. No one who knows the job from inside will
imagine that we can add much in new subjects, nor
interfere much in the scope of the old.

But my point is that so much *is* relevant. Take
Theology: A few days ago three of us were talking
—a university professor of Theology, an ex-India
missionary, and I. It was about a young minister
engaged in missionary training who wanted to continue some theological study to 'keep his hand in ',
so to speak. 'What courses have you which he
might attend? '

'I have one class of more mature students which
he might join,' said the professor. ' We are reading
Origen: last term *De Principiis,* next term *Contra
Celsum*—if you think that is relevant.'

'Relevant!' said my ex-Indian colleague—and a distant look came into his eyes as when a man thinks of his first love. 'I worked through it when I was up in Bangalore. It seemed so up to date that I went out forthwith and tried it section by section in bazaar-preaching. You remember—the absurdity of the Christians' claims to knowledge of God! They are like worms in the corner of the dunghill, yet they cry, "To us God reveals all things, and with us alone He has fellowship." That was exactly how caste-Hindus were mocking the simple faith of outcaste Christians.'[1]

'I wonder what year that was,' said I. 'In Canton in 1927 at the height of the anti-Christian movement, I was putting my Chinese theologues on to it, to show them that all this stuff ("They say do not examine, only believe") might be the latest from Moscow, but it was the worn-out witticisms of eighteen centuries ago, forgotten and lost except for this sufficient answer in Christian apology.'[2]

How much of it is relevant! But the relevance is in danger of being missed. Students, whether impatient of their academic training or absorbed in it, often need reminding that it is not merely academic. Teachers, rightly concerned with academic standards, may overlook the help which they should be able to give in relating this subject to life. From my own classroom work I am persuaded that the main justification for the lecture method is the chance which it gives to communicate enthusiasm for a subject. It

[1] More fully worked out in *The Ancient Church and Modern India,* now unhappily out of print. The writer, Professor G. E. Phillips, is the colleague to whom I refer above.
[2] Mentioned with more detail p. 80 above.

is justified as a means of communicating information too, when the material is original and unpublished, or when approach or arrangement are startlingly new. But if it were only information—who does not remember in his own student days a general preference for books? For one thing, there need not be such a scramble to get it down! But enthusiasm—that can never be passed on so well as by a living medium. And, by the same token, enthusiasm kindles best in me as something comes to life under my hands.

Or take Biblical Studies: I was a member of a group studying mass movements. We had a specialist on the subject, straight from the field. The rest of us were missionaries or ex-missionaries. There was one Old Testament professor present, a man with no missionary experience. I thought he might feel rather out of it. But at one point in our conversations he looked up with a smile and said, ' You know the whole of my subject might be described under the title " How a mass movement became the Church ", or " From the Tribes in Egypt to the Ecclesia of God". *That is what the Old Testament is about.*'

Some of us, who were well taught in this subject, belonged to a student generation which was so intent on questions of date and authorship that we sometimes missed the element of timelessness, that in the Scriptures which belongs to all time. A man may come to sound scholarship without having come to use the Old Testament aright. Perhaps this temper in our generation explains the fact that in so many of the Younger Churches, where the Old Testament is not misused, it is neglected. Here at home many people know little more than the hero stories (of which they think vaguely, as they do of Jack the Giant-killer), with perhaps a few verses from the Psalms. They have no idea of the unfolding of a connected purpose, no knowledge of 'what the Old Testament is about'.

In student discussion groups, we sometimes stumbled across things not yet mentioned in the classroom. I remember one such group over twenty years ago, where we were already wondering whether Indian Christians might not find their Psalms in the *Bhagavadgita,* Chinese their Wisdom Literature in the Confucian Classics—an old testament of their own, to which *the* New Testament, theirs and ours, might come as natural fulfilment. We did hear of Marcion in another classroom, but we did not learn to associate his ancient heresy with our new enlightenment.[1] Historical Theology, as well as Old Testament study, might have benefited in liveliness if we had.

I suppose κήρυγμα (preaching) has become *the* central word of New Testament study. And it no longer concerns just a few sample sermon outlines in the Acts received at second hand, and suspected of being the narrator's composition, not the Apostles'. We know now that the apostolic preaching determined much of the form in which records of our Lord's deeds and words have come down to us in the Gospels. It is the burden of the Epistles which are but the Apostles' written representatives. And 'apostle' means 'missionary'. Linguistically the exact equivalent in Latin of the Greek ἀπόστολος would be 'e-missus'. 'Emissary' is so near to

---

[1] See p. 110, and footnote, above.

'missionary' that no word of modern usage, and we may add no task in the modern Church, is so truly apostolic. The New Testament is the first, it must ever remain the chief, missionary handbook.

I have left Church History till last. In many ways this subject is the most relevant of all. The following illustration may focus light which every chapter in this book is meant to throw on the teaching and study of this subject:

Gibbon scoffs at Tertullian[1] for leaning over the battlements of heaven and imagining its joys the sweeter because of contrast with the torments of the damned. We have been used to agreeing with Gibbon here—at least we sympathized with Gibbon's criticism better than we understood Tertullian's severity. Was it not a species of religious sadism? But now, after listening to eye-witnesses' accounts of horrors in the occupation of Poland, after talking with pastors who have come twisted and broken from concentration camps, after conning a war-map of fifteen hundred miles of trampled frontiers and bloody harvest fields—we understand. We should ever be afraid of it in ourselves, this righteous indignation, even as we are afraid of the wrath of God. They are akin. Tertullian is a century after the writer of the Book of the Revelation, with its songs of triumph over the Beast which is bound and cast into Hell. The Revelation is half a century (or would you say more?) after One who spoke awful words of a great millstone and the depth of the sea. We feel ourselves nearer to the early centuries because we have suddenly

[1] *Decline and Fall of the Roman Empire*, Vol. II, pp. 26f. The reference is to Tertullian's *De Spectaculis*, 30.

realized what it is to come face to face with human nature unredeemed, with a society unleavened, pagan to the core and closed against His gospel.

We have been plunged back into the pagan world with a shock. This immediately affects our Theology (the wrath of God), our Bible Studies (The Revelation, Matthew xviii, etc., as above), but most of all our Church History. Second-century Tertullian not only leans over the battlements of heaven; we now know that he stands shoulder to shoulder with us looking out upon just such a world. But if this is suddenly true in these few respects of you, it is always true, and in almost all respects, of the missionary.

Undergraduates in China are as disrespectful as our own about some of their studies. The subject of History is called *sz-chi*. *Sz* means ' historical ' and *chi* means ' records ' or ' memory '. A favourite pun is to refer to another *sz* which means ' death ' or ' dead '. So ' history ' comes to mean ' dead records '. Sometimes, as examinations approach and dates are being crammed, they say the phrase *sz-chi*, at the same time passing a hand over a weary brow: ' Death to the memory! ' But that is not history: Polybius says, ' The soundest education and training for life ' —life, not death, I would have you notice—' is the study of history, for there is no more ready corrective of conduct than knowledge of the past.' I cannot teach the first four centuries as dead—because as a missionary I have *been there*. Some think that ' Younger Churches ' is nothing more than a modern pedantic way of talking about the mission field. One purpose of this book is to show that it is a modern way of saying ' Early Church '. It is in our contemporary expansion of the Church that Church History comes to life. This thesis has already been fully developed in Chapter IV. A few of its practical results for education need to be mentioned here.

It is recognized that we need a new missionary appeal to the churches. There are lands still largely unevangelized. There remains some pioneering to be done. But the money we raise and the men we recruit are more likely to be used for the upbuilding of churches already established. The remaining pioneer work will most of it be done, not by the foreign missionary, but by nationals of those churches. The romance attached to the missionary as explorer, or adventurer, or someone who went somewhere or did something (even preached the gospel) for the first time, is an anachronism. In any case it was a false romance which glorified a mere accident of his environment rather than the essentials of his calling. It is truer to declare that the Church's heroic age has come again, and that Older and Younger Churches, because of their unity in the World-wide Church, have the privilege of being in it together. That should be the missionary appeal for to-day. This conception is of immense importance in theological education.

The Madras Conference recognized that we are in need of new emphases in missionary training. Among the functions of the missionary there set forth[1] I have already drawn attention to one item which could not be expected in the period of the pioneer. As we recognize that ours is a different day, so we should know the new day's demands: 'To embody and transmit the

[1] *The Life of the Church*, Tambaram Madras Series, Vol. IV, p. 253.

experience of the Universal Church.' Indeed the
findings go on to mention the central place of this
subject in the training of the missionary :

'We call attention of all theological and missionary
training institutions to the importance for missionaries
of the study of Church History—for guidance and warning from the past, for the development of a right church-
consciousness in the Younger Church, and for the
approach to church union.'[1]

In the article which follows, I have said :

'Most important of all is the strengthening of the
connexion between the historic Church and the missionary. He will go to a land where everything Christian is
young, and where nothing is needed more than the
steadying influence of the past. His life-work will
be with the questions—those vital problems, conflicts,
failures, opportunities, choices—with which the Tambaram findings deal. He needs to know that, so far
from being new, many of these very things form land-
marks in the progress of the Church, and that history is
rich in guidance and warnings from which he may
profit. He will be lonely, and in need of all which may
help him to know that he belongs to a grand and glorious
succession.'[2]

The Younger Churches need nothing so much as a
sense of the past. Hitherto nothing has been weaker
in our missionary contribution. This must be set
right. The place to set it right is in education.

Not least is this conception important, because this
is where the subject comes to life. Indeed I am
persuaded that it is near to this spot that the whole
of theological study might come to a new relevance,
not by addition of new subjects to an already over-

[1] *Ibid.*, p. 257.   [2] *Ibid.*, p. 259.

burdened curriculum, but by the addition to every subject of a background—that background the living Church stretching down through the centuries and reaching out over a needy world.

CHAPTER VIII

THE CHURCH—WORLD-DENYING AND
WORLD-AFFIRMING

IF 'Education for World-Churchmanship' be our
theme, it is clear that we must give more thought
to the relation of the Church to the world. In St.
John's Gospel xvii. 6, you will find one description
of the Church: 'The men whom Thou gavest me
out of the world.' Then from verse 11 there comes
a striking change:

'I am no more in the world, but these are in the
world. . . . (18) As Thou hast sent Me, even so have I
also sent them into the world. . . . (20) (Others) shall
believe on Me through their word . . . (21) that the
world may believe. . . .'

There in the words of our Lord's high-priestly prayer
you have a glimpse of two aspects of the Church:
First, it is the community of the redeemed, who are
saved out of the world. Second, it is the instrument
for the fulfilling of God's purposes in the world, influencing the world's life, and working towards its
salvation.

Recognition of these two aspects is a key which
opens understanding of large sections of Church
History. It is one thing for our Lord—or His closest

followers—to set out these two complimentary aspects. It is another for later generations of Christians to hold the balance between them. The one is intensive, narrow and world-denying. The other is extensive, broad and world-affirming. We need not be surprised that the Church has always tended to become lop-sided: probably we ourselves, immediately the contrast was mentioned, began to face it from the 'either . . . or' point of view. In the Gospel it is 'both . . . and'.

The Church of the early centuries is pre-eminently the Church saved out of the world. Christianity is a despised minority movement. As in so large a part of the world to-day, to be a Christian means to have to separate oneself from many activities of family and clan, society and city—household gods, temple dues, idol feasts, and the taint of paganism which runs through social life. 'Come ye out from among them and be ye separate.' The spirit of such a separate community is likely to be exalted, its fellowship close, its ideals high. Its danger is from an excessive other-worldliness.

Take as example Ignatius, Bishop of Antioch, now (c. 110) a captive under escort on his way to Rome. He sends a letter ahead pleading with the Christians of the capital not to seek means for his acquittal—rather would he embrace the opportunity of martyr-dom and go to the beasts in the Colosseum:

'I beseech you, be not " an unseasonable kindness " to me. Suffer me to be eaten by the beasts, through whom I can attain to God. I am God's wheat, and I am ground by the teeth of wild beasts, that I may be found pure bread of Christ. Rather entice the wild beasts that they

may become my tomb, and leave no trace of my body,
that when I fall asleep I be not burdensome to any. Then
shall I be truly a disciple of Jesus Christ. . . . From Syria
to Rome I am fighting with wild beasts. . . . I long for
the beasts that are prepared for me. . . . Let there come
on me fire, and cross, and struggles with wild beasts,
cutting and tearing asunder, rackings of bones, mangling
of limbs, crushing of my whole body, cruel tortures of
the devil, may I but attain to Jesus Christ! . . . Suffer
me to receive the pure light. When I have come thither
I shall become a man. Suffer me to follow the example
of the passion of my God.'[1]

Compare that attitude with St. Paul as we see him
in the Imprisonment Epistles.[2] Do you not feel that
there is something almost neurotic about Ignatius?
Yes, neurosis is always just round the corner in such
a heroic age. I felt similarly about many of the
continental delegates at the Madras Conference
of 1938, especially those who came from the Con-
fessional Church. Of course we admired them. I
kneel in veneration at the feet of Ignatius, saint and
martyr. But when I hear men lightly say that it
might be good for our churches here in Britain if we
had to suffer for the faith, I say no. The heroic age
has its dangers, as great as those of the period of peace.

From 313, the Edict of Milan, onwards we enter a
different period. The Christians who 'turn the world
upside down' have turned it until the cross, the
gibbet of the Roman world, has taken the place of
the eagles of victory on the standards of the legions.
The despised minority is recognized as contributing
to the life of the Empire a religion which can 'set in

---

[1] *Ignatius to the Romans*, iv.-vi.
[2] e.g. Philippians i. 23-26, ' in a strait betwixt the two '.

order the body of the world, now labouring under grievous sickness '.

The danger here is entirely other than that of the first period: central in the life of the world, the Church is threatened with worldliness. The danger is clear in the forty years of peace (210-250), before the final persecutions. Cyprian, Bishop of Carthage, tells us that

' Everyone was busy getting rich, and forgetting what was the conduct of believers under the apostles. . . . Priests were lacking in devotion, deacons in the wholeness of their faith; there were no works of mercy, no discipline of manners. Men wore their beards disfigured. Women made up their faces with lipstick and rouge, and put a false colour over their hair.'[1]

Some of it sounds remarkably familiar. So do complaints about marriage with unbelievers, pride of place which cools the former warmth of fellowship, factions and quarrels which divide the hitherto close community, and the worldly employments of the clergy—even of the bishops.[1]

Or take this later letter, of Jerome's, which belongs to the dreadful time when the Dark Ages were closing in upon our Western world, sealing the doom of an unholy Empire—and, some thought, of an unworthy Church :

' The world sinks into ruin. Yes, but, shameful to say, our sins still live and flourish. The renowned city, the capital of the Empire, is swallowed up in one tremendous fire; and there is no part of the earth where Romans are not in exile. Churches once held sacred are now but

[1] *De Lapsis*, pp. 5, 6.

heaps of dust and ashes. Yet we have our minds set on the idea of gain. We live as though we were going to die to-morrow; yet we build as though we were going to live always in this world. Our walls shine with gold, our ceilings also and the capitals of our pillars; yet Christ dies before our doors, naked and hungry, in the persons of His poor.'[1]

How like the ruin of which we hear abroad, some of the desolation which we see at home, the plight of modern refugees everywhere—and the persistent worldliness of our own day though the world is going to pieces. No wonder Jerome rebukes it. That is the danger—worldliness.

It is no accident that it is from the time of the Church's triumph in the Mediterranean world that monasticism becomes a significant movement. Instead of mob opposition against the Christian community, there is a mass movement into it. To be a Christian means not persecution, but preferment. The Church has come out of the catacombs, to occupy (it is the cathedral of Rome to this day) the imperial palace of the Lateran. The terminology of the medieval Church is a sign of the ' either . . . or ' mentality which now begins to prevail. The main part of the Church is called secular (i.e. ' in the world '). An exceptional minority is termed *religious*. It is a strange and limiting use of the word when ' religious ' has come to mean ' monastic '. It is an index of the way in which this movement has captured the imagination of the pious, until its new, strange and rival expression of religion comes to be accepted as *the* expression. Monasticism is a revival of the other-

[1] *Epistles*, cxxviii.

K

worldly aspect. It begins as a leaving not only of the world, but of the Church which is in the world, a protest against its compromise, its abuses, its nominalness, its too easy taking for granted of religion. It builds up another system alongside, at first unrelated to, in many ways even opposed to, that which has come to be accepted as the traditional Church. And the Church, instead of saying farewell to the solitary and the monk, enlarges its boundaries to contain them. It happens again and again with each monastic revival. And so right through the Middle Ages two antithetical expressions of Christianity, the secular one world-affirming, the regular one world-denying, stand side by side, become related, act and react upon each other, as two different—we may even say opposite—aspects of the same Church.

So we come to the modern age. It affords good opportunity to shock the more timidly Protestant of one's brethren by dwelling upon the fact (is it not a fact?) that our post-Reformation denominations are the modern equivalent of pre-Reformation monastic orders.[1] Those of us who are most offended at the idea of a spiritual ancestry by way of the monks are also those who shrink from the worldly Church, the grandee bishop, the nominal allegiance to a born-so Christianity which is little more than the religious side of worldly society. This means, of course, that the less we like the monks, the more we belong to that essentially monastic protest against the Church-in-the-world, a dilemma from which there is no escape. But seriously: of all our unhappy divisions, those which really count are between parts of the

[1] See pp. 45f. above.

Church which have carried on the medieval tradition of the secular Church, and those whose Protestantism has been in the form of a recapturing of the sect ideal.

The fact that some Protestant communions have, as really as the medieval Church, attempted to combine the two aspects, does not disprove my thesis but illustrates it. Perhaps it is best seen in that tradition which begins in Geneva and finds its full development in Scotland. Of all the lands of the Reformation most was done there to maintain both the centrality in society and the being saved out of the world, the national Church and the sect ideal. Yet was it not the difficulty of keeping up the synthesis which caused the bitter divisions of later years, and which makes their healing, begun in 1929, so lengthy a process? With regard to England there is no doubt. Between the Established Church and the Dissenters (I use the name for the sake of its history), the division which really divides is here. Most denominations traditionally represent one of these two aspects to the exclusion of the other. Individual apprehension of religion may be similarly one-sided. The psychologist talks about extravert and introvert. So might we. We are all engaged in building a new world, all outward service; or we are all withdrawal from the world, all inner devotion. Something of the same sort comes between our rival theologies. Two of the strongest cross-currents which ruffled the surface of discussions at Madras—a few years ago it would have been Modernism and Fundamentalism, but in 1938 these were hardly heard of!—were what might be called Activism, and Quietism: Activism, a Christianity which seeks the social implications of the gospel, works for the redemption of society, believes that the Kingdom of God is to be built up from among the earthly kingdoms; Quietism, a Christianity which despairs of this world order as being under the condemnation of God, and waits for a salvation which is from above. The first was often labelled 'American Christianity' and profoundly pitied by those who affixed the label because it was optimistic. The other might have been labelled 'made in Germany'. It fitted the mood of despair as the more sensitive of our continental brethren saw the pit opening at their feet. But of course the difference is not dependent upon anything so modern as post-Munich unsettlement. It belongs to the other-worldly, i.e. the monastic, reaction typical of continental Protestantism.

Now, you may say, you are getting tied up in this too-involved theory: 'American Christianity' is surely just as Protestant, indeed much of it is obviously more Protestant, than that of Germany. That is just the point: it belongs to the 'saved-out-of-the-world' reaction. Originally it was, and if true to its tradition it would remain, other-worldly. But there has come a reaction to the reaction. It should have meant a return to the Church-in-the-world emphasis, the Church central in society, saving society. But alas! it has not meant any greater degree of churchmanship. That which to this type of Christian is central in the world is not the Church, but a vague disembodied Christianity, a diffused Christian idealism, a 'social gospel'.

That which brought the two extremes together at Madras, as you will see if you refer to that excellent theological statement, *The Faith by which the*

Church Lives,[1] was that which I believe is the only thing ever to do so: the emergence of a higher churchmanship—one which gets back from all our periodic 'either . . . or' solutions to the 'both . . . and' from which we started in St. John's Gospel. Here is a summary of what the Madras Conference has to say: The Kingdom is both within and beyond this world. Our churches, feeble and divided as they are, do enshrine the true Church. The Church—yes, the Church visible—is growing in universality and in unity, even while the world is being threatened with dissolution. We *are* one. The Church is even now the actualization of its own message, a foretaste of the redeemed family of God which He has purposed all mankind should be. . . .

Why have I cantered down the centuries and landed in Madras and all the while kept up this refrain about the two aspects of the Church? That it has something to do with the World-Church we see, because we landed in Madras. That it has anything to do with education for World-Churchmanship (which was where we started) may not be so obvious.

First is the need for a higher churchmanship. The swing away from that other-worldliness which belongs to the spiritual ancestry of most of us is so serious a thing, not because it has made us care too much for this world. That was a needed corrective. We must have a social gospel. Did we ever need one more than in these days of *rapprochement* with Russia—when the possibility of a *rapprochement* between the Soviets and the Church is surely to be kept in mind? We need an international

[1] Tambaram Madras Series, Vol. I, pp. 186ff.

gospel, never more than in the day of reconstruction which will dawn upon a ruined world.
It is serious because so many of us have no bit of
the eternal reaching down into the temporal. We
do not know that the Church Triumphant has as
its colony the Church Militant here on earth. We
need that Church, not other-worldly, but supra-
mundane, as solid core for all our idealisms, nucleus
of all our hopes for a New Order.

When I was a student, just after the last war, it
was our fashion to be unconventional. For theological students that meant unecclesiastical. It was
not my training, but pressure of experience afterwards which persuaded me otherwise. I do not mean
that I came to abhor any less the clerical voice, the
professional or 'bedside' manner. I do mean that
I came to be uneasy about that current Protestant
blasphemy which describes the visible Church as
'organized religion', with the superior assumption that
the vaguer one is in that regard the safer for all of us.
I mean a return to the apostolic faith in ' the Church
which is His body, the fulfilment of Him who is
being out-and-out fulfilled '. After experience of the
work of the Church abroad I would not send out any
of your hazy idealists—for international relations,
social uplift, rural reconstruction, and the rest—no,
nor your zealot for mere individual conversions
either. Unless work is Church-centred, it will not
endure.

In the last chapter I illustrated from each of the
four main subjects how relevant to *World*-Churchman-
ship a theological education is. We need now to
go over them again with the question of *churchman-*

ship in mind.   Theology: I find that the cycle of
three annual subjects for the B.D. degree at London
is not very different from that of a generation ago—
Man, Sin, and Grace; Incarnation and the Trinity;
the Work of Christ.   Is the heart of Theology all
there?   In discussing the handling of material with
one New Testament professor, he told me that when
he was a student he attended an exposition of St.
John's Gospel.   They spent three lectures on the word
εὐαγγέλιον, and at the end of the term had got as
far as chapter one, verse four.   Next term the syllabus
bade them move on to pastures new.   Are we treat-
ing doctrine similarly—never getting so far down
the creed as 'I believe in the Holy Ghost, the holy
Catholic Church, the communion of saints'?

A group of us was discussing what was the central
theme of the Old Testament.   The righteousness of
God, said one.   The development of the idea of the
personality of God, said another.   I forget what others
said. My mind immediately leapt to the people of
God, the congregation, the *ecclesia,* of which the
middle wall of partition is now broken down, and
we are no more strangers and foreigners, but fellow-
citizens with the saints and of the household of God.
Was not Augustine right—this is central in all history?[1]

New Testament: I heard an Indian bishop tell the
way that an enquirer from Hinduism came to seek
Christian baptism.   Reading the New Testament without help or guidance, he soon saw what it was about.
The picture of our Lord in the Gospels fascinated
him.   The passion and death of Christ moved him.

[1] See p. 26 above.

'Then he read on . . . and felt he had entered into a new world. In the Gospels it was Jesus, His works, and His suffering. In the Acts . . . what the disciples did and thought and taught had taken the place that Christ had occupied. The Church continued where Jesus left off at His death. "Therefore," said this man to me, "I must belong to the Church that carries on the life of Christ." '[1]

Have these things been hidden from the wise and understanding, even while they are revealed unto babes?

Church History: It may appear that this subject is necessarily concerned with churchmanship if it is taught at all. And yet a senior minister, defending the attitude to 'organized religion' which I have attacked as a blasphemy, said in a letter to me, 'The more I read the history of the Church, the more I marvel that a visible Church has persisted.' Who, I should like to ask, was the blind guide who tried to put his feet upon the path? It is like being so dismayed at the humiliation of our Lord's earthly life as to doubt the reality of the first incarnation. 'The Church which is His body' is no chance phrase, once dropped in too daring allegory, and never to be taken up again. 'In Christ' is *the* great phrase of the New Testament, occurring over eighty times. If I mistake not, it is to this Body, as outward and visible sign of an otherwise wholly mystical experience, that its reference is made.

Second, is the need for a wider churchmanship: When we think of the Younger Churches it is usually of small minorities in a pagan environment,

[1] Tambaram Madras Series, Vol. VII, p. 40, an address by the Bishop of Dornakal.

separate and self-regarding, struggling to keep themselves unspotted from the world. That is one side of
the picture—but only one. The other has been there
even from the beginning. William Carey went to
India in 1793 from the pastorate of a small Baptist
church in Leicester. You might expect him to have
taken with him only the sect ideal. Had he represented his more immediate environment, belonged
to nothing wider than his most recent ancestry, it
would have been so.[1] But in the providence of God
Carey was able to dream of the Church as central
to a new culture which would win its way in every
land of the East. In Serampore he put up a building
very different from the barn-like chapels of eighteenth-century nonconformity. His college stood for
education under the shadow of the Church just as
truly as did any medieval university. Indeed in the
year 1827 it was granted a charter by the King of
Denmark, to become the first university in India,
and to remain the only Christian one to this day.[2]

The modern missionary movement has continued
to develop on these broad lines: In India the grant-
in-aid system has meant that missions have been able
to undertake immense educational work. In China,
without any aid from Government, a Christian school
system crowned by no less than thirteen Christian
universities—surely outdoing the Church of the
Middle Ages!—for long set the pace for all modern-

[1] 'It is surely our duty to forget the distinctions which divide
society in England, and to make common cause. . . . Every public
institution, aiming at India's betterment, ought to be constructed
on so broad a basis as to invite the aid of all denominations.'
Quoted by S. Pearce Carey in *William Carey*, p. 352.
[2] There are many Christian colleges, affiliated with universities.
Serampore is the only one with its own charter.

style education and produced many of the upbuilders
of the new national life. Now it is Africa's turn:
British colonial governments there have decided to
work for the most part through the missions rather
than undertake an independent policy of education.
Once again the Church is seizing its opportunity to
claim the rising generation.

Educational work is but one illustration—the
natural one to which to turn if one begins with
Carey. But the main-stream of the Younger
Churches' life is similarly wide. I referred before
to the local church as ' not a very impressive affair '.[1]
But out of the Edinburgh Conference of 1910 there
began a growth, delayed for several years by the
Great War, but since continued—that of the Christian
Councils. To-day there are the National Christian
Councils of India, Burma and Ceylon, of Siam, of
China, and of Japan, and regional councils in the
Near East, the Philippines, Latin America, and South
Africa. The small struggling local church is not all:
there is already a Church with a national (or regional)
significance. Great movements on a nation-wide scale
—literacy, rural reconstruction, co-operatives, public
health—some of them a permanent contribution to
the needs of society, have been begun by the Church,
or depend largely upon the Church's co-operation
with the State.

In all these ways, without the Church having
reached the strength or dignity of a State religion,
there is in many lands of the Younger Churches an
' in-the-world ' relationship which is due—overdue—
for recognition. Such recognition would involve a

[1] p. 66 above.

radical change in the whole matter of churchmanship for many whose religious life continues as though nothing of this had happened. Let me illustrate from actual cases:

A man goes out to the service of the Church in West Africa, or among the hill people of Burma or the aborigines of West China. He finds a church vastly different from that of the English suburb where he grew up. Rather will he be reminded of the Bishop Ulfilas, who in the fourth century adapted Greek characters to fit the sounds spoken by the Goths, and so made the Bible the ancestor of all German literature; or of the Bishop of Arran in Persia, who in the sixth century used Syriac script for writing Tatar sounds, the first writing known to many peoples of Central Asia, and traceable in Mongol and Manchu letters to this day. Here again in this modern world the missionary has devised an alphabet for people who had no literature, that he might translate the Bible. But not the Bible only: lo, within a generation there are young Christians from these truly illiterate tribes already beginning to enter the learned professions. 'That will make them more like his English suburb,' did you say? No indeed: it is stepping back into the Dark Ages when the only centre of all culture was the Church.

With one young man who had been brought up solely on the ideal of the 'gathered Church', 'the worthiest be they never so few', I had a long talk about adjustments which he needed to make in his thinking. He was going to a part of India where his Society, men of similar upbringing, had been God's instruments for a great ingathering. Thousands of outcastes had come over—not as individuals, for it was before the dawn of individualism with them, but under their headmen; converted as a community even as our fathers were when Augustine's mission won the King of Kent, or when Aidan evangelized Northumbria.

I visited a mission compound where there are schools for boys, training for men, who will go out to the service of the Church; parallel institutions for girls and women; a printing-press which enlightens the countryside; weaving and other handicrafts, which help to uplift the standards of village life; a hospital with patients and out-patients from a wide area, and public-health workers going out to cleanse the sources of disease; all this and more. It has been called, and indeed must be, one of the biggest mission compounds in the world. In the middle, inspiration of it all, the meaning of these multifarious services, is a great church. As I saw its towers above the scrub of the jungle, I thought of the towers of Ely or of Crowland rising over the fens. An abbey in the Middle Ages, with its almoner and guest-master, its scriptorium, library and school, its bake-house, brew-house, mill, and manor farm—at its best, an influence to uplift the life of a whole countryside, and the abbey church at its heart—this is its closest parallel. The compound is the property of the Methodist Missionary Society. It is far from the Methodism of the village chapel, the suburban church, or even the city mission-hall, here in England.

There are missionaries of the Society of Friends who find on their foreign station that the meeting-house is the only parish church—and of an amazingly wide parish. I have an acquaintance in Africa who has been known to argue fiercely for Free Church principles. But when you ask about his work, you find he is a veritable Archbishop Laud to the local king—in influence, I mean, not in the unwisdom of its exercise. In Nanking, at the time of the launching of the New Life Movement, I heard of a missionary who was attached to what was virtually a Government department. He belongs to a society supported by those who used to call themselves Independents and stood most firmly for complete separation of Church and State. So one might go on.

It is nothing new. Indeed that is just the point— it is not so new as our denominational differentiations. Sharing the missionary task inevitably means going into a stage of Church life which belongs further back. Negative elements in our denominational heritage, due to protests against abuses in our own Middle Ages, must not be allowed to limit our freedom in going in to possess a new land in the name of Christ and of His holy Church. It is not, as die-hards of the old controversies might have us believe, denying our birthright. It is claiming something wider than denominational heritage, something more common, or, if you will, more catholic.

I have already quoted those startling words from the Madras findings about the function of the modern missionary: 'To embody and transmit the experience of the Universal Church'. Training for World-Churchmanship must be concerned with that. Are we doing anything about it?

I confess that I was sent out to China a narrow denominationalist with little experience and not much sympathy beyond the bounds of my own communion. Towards the end of my period of service I was visited by one of our distinguished ministers, who in conversation asked me, 'Has your experience made you feel that our Church has something to contribute which China cannot afford to miss?' Without hesitation I replied, 'Yes. . . . There is only one thing of which I am more sure: ours alone would be a partial emphasis and an insufficient contribution.'

Here is something which we ought to recognize. It is true of the monastic orders of the Middle Ages, and equally true of the denominations of our own day. There comes a revival. It throws into clear relief the abuses of the unrevived Church. It brings back forgotten, lost, or overlaid essentials of true Christian living. It starts white-hot, like molten metal —but that cannot last. It settles down, flows into a conventional mould—an old one already handy, or one made for the occasion, cools, hardens, and . . . there you are, waiting for another revival.

The monks, we saw, came as a reaction against the worldliness of the Church, the nominalness of religion which in extending its influence had compromised its standards, the born-so, take-it-for-granted attitude to Christianity in the third and fourth centuries. The reaction was successful. It attracted men. It became popular. They flocked to the monastery, brought gifts to the monastery, bequeathed lands to the monastery. The men who had sought solitude found themselves the objects of popular esteem. Those who had given themselves to apostolic poverty were surrounded by prosperous estates. Those whose protest had been for the sake of an absolute standard, themselves inevitably bowed to compromise. A movement which had been a return to other-worldliness was fast becoming as worldly as the secular Church from which it had reacted.

The same is true of later revivals. When I attend a Methodist church there is no guarantee that I shall be able to say to myself, ' Ah, these are the children of the eighteenth-century revival.' The fact is there are as many barren patches in this as in any other section of the field. The Congregationalist believes in a ' gathered church '. Not because of birth or as an assumed part of one's cultural environment is he a church-member, but because of individual conviction. His son may be in as much danger of merely inheriting his denomination as is the son of anyone else. The Quaker rebels against the shams of outward form. Then a leading Quaker asks me to preach at his meeting, and *pretends* that my sermon is unpremeditated—no, not because he expects to deceive anybody, but because formlessness has itself become an artificial form. Still more, when one takes these (and other) partial emphases to lands which have never known the general background against which they still have some meaning in the West, it is then that one realizes how poverty-stricken some of them can be, how partial, and ineffective.

Most of us keep near our telephone a list of the numbers which we have used most. I believe in such a card; indeed I can carry through most of my regular duties, only occasionally having to turn elsewhere. But I do not disclaim interest when the the telephone company sends me a copy of the directory. Training for World-Churchmanship does not mean disregarding denominational distinctions. Whatever the way by which religion has 'got through' to you, of course you must keep a list of the numbers. And it is from that list—the heart of your own experience—that you have most chance of helping others. My plea for a wider churchmanship means that, as well as the card, you claim possession of the whole directory.

In these days of the Ecumenical Movement, when schemes of reunion are coming—and coming first, note, from the lands of the Younger Churches,[1] when the time is ripe for changes for which our congregations have not begun to be prepared, and never will except through a vastly different ministry—it matters.

To return to the two aspects of the Church with which we started: I came to recognize that my own spiritual heritage did belong to one side of the picture. Indeed I went on to become acutely conscious of, and distressed by, my denominational one-sidedness. Then I came to the positive solution of accepting that, as representing our distinctive contribution to the reunited Church of the future. And at the same time I began *to covet the opposite gift*, which I found represented in similar strength (one-sidedness too, one might say) by one of the other denominations.

'Be tenderly affectioned one to another, in honour preferring one another.'
'. . . Each counting other better than himself.'[2]

When such feelings have been developed among

[1] See, e.g., W. J. Noble, *Church Union in South India.*
[2] Romans xii. 10, Philippians ii. 3.

members of different branches of the Church, and their intelligent expression has taken the place of ignorant beating of the denominational drum, a large measure of Church reunion will be in sight.

But it will not come by any happy accident.

CHAPTER IX

CHURCHMANSHIP IN THE UNIVERSAL CHURCH

IN the creed commonly called Nicene we repeat the words 'I believe one Holy, Catholic, and Apostolic Church'. It is time to enquire whether in our churchmanship these words have come to their true meaning. In training for churchmanship do we lead men to see, and to serve, a Church which is catholic and apostolic? Apostolic—I want them to be conscious of a succession. Catholic—lifted above all partial emphases, I want comprehension.

Let us begin with the first, *Apostolic*, or (we will not join the two into one phrase, or how should I be the one to discuss it?) belonging to a *succession*. An increasing number of us try to live keeping in mind, more prominent than our denominational consciousness, the fact that we are servants of the Universal Church. But of course one cannot belong to the Universal Church without belonging to one part of it. There is no other way in. It is of no use having nice feelings about the universal if you have no relationship to the local, or thinking beautiful thoughts about the ideal if you are not hard at work in the real. St. Jerome pillories such comfortable romanticists so early as the year 400, when he mocks the patronage of religion which is now being afforded by ladies of fashionable society in Rome: ' After an immoderate supper, they go to bed to dream of the Apostles.'[1]

I have not been dreaming of the Apostles but doing a definite task. I do belong to a part. It may not be your part. That is what makes the subject of the Church so difficult. So let me state a general principle: if you accept *the historic faith*, and, accepting it, act in accordance with the discipline of that part of the Church which brought you to its acceptance, then I believe that you ought to be able to claim that you belong to the Church—to all of it, and that all of it belongs to you: ' I believe one Holy, Catholic, and Apostolic Church.' That is what the words of the creed mean to me.

Nor does it matter one whit that the Roman Church, half Christendom, cannot acknowledge me; or that among non-Roman Churches there are some, both right and left, who find occasion of stumbling. It is for them to fix the limits of their own churchmanship, not mine. I can lay my claim to be heir of all the ages because of the faith, the full New Testament faith *which has come down all the ages,* and which I hold, or (should I say?) holds me. With Bishop Jewel I am ready to deny to the Romans that

' all antiquity and a continual assent of all ages doth make on their side; . . . we are yesterday's work, until these last few years never heard of.'[2]

With him I may, on occasion, be ready to retort,

' Though faith fall, so they say, yet succession must hold, for unto succession God hath bound the Holy Ghost!

[1] *Epistles*, xxii.
[2] Jewel, *Apology for the Church of England*, written in 1562.

. . . They are not always godly that succeed the godly.
. . . It is not sufficient to claim succession of place; it
behoveth us rather to have succession of doctrine.'[1]

There is a succession about which I have no doubts
and I will not let the doubts of others disturb me.

Some of us may have been brought up to think far
otherwise. More of us, perhaps, may not have been
brought up at all, but 'just growed up'—in this
regard, I mean! For religious education, whether in
church or school, for the most part stops with the
teaching of scripture. It should go on to link
the Acts, which is the first book of Church History, the
Epistles, which may be called the inner life of
the Early Church, and the Revelation, which is its
triumph song, with the Church now as it has come
down to us, even the church which stands at the
corner of our street. No wonder the small boy said
to his teacher after the scripture lesson, ' Gee! but
God was a lot more exciting in those days, wasn't
He? ' The answer is (or should have been), ' No '.
Our Lord promised His disciples,

' He that believeth on me, the works that I do shall he
do also; and greater works than these shall he do.'[2]

That promise has been literally fulfilled in His
Church. The greatest of all these works belongs to
the Church in the last three generations.

If popular education suffers this lack, much of
theological education leaves one wondering what the
doctrine of the Church can be which has given rise
to anything so warped and stunted.

[1] Jewel, *Defence of the Apology.*
[2] John xiv. 12.

CHURCHMANSHIP IN UNIVERSAL CHURCH 165

Perhaps you think that I am exaggerating our short-comings. Again, this is not theory, but the result of experience as a missionary. When I was set to teach Church History in a theological college in China, I found that in all my text-books, the term used to represent ' Protestantism ' was ' *san chiao* '. That means ' new religion '. I used to tell new students in their first class that if they used that term in my classroom I should count it a capital offence. New religion indeed! In that case where were my subject and I? The important questions to ask, however, are, What view of the Church is implied? and, Where did it come from? Missionary predecessors who fixed such a term must have got wrong not only their Church History, but their Theology, and New Testament—yes, and Old Testament too, for if a man does not know that the roots of the Church are there he may as well not know the Old Testament at all. You may imagine that meeting so surprising a situation I made what enquiries I could. You may guess that I enquired most about the teaching of my own subject in the experience of my fellow-missionaries.

I found it to be the widespread fashion to treat Church History somewhat seriously for the first five centuries (451 seems to be a favourite date), and then to take a leap. Where you come down to earth again depends upon denominational taste: Lutherans begin from the monk of Wittenberg and his Ninety-five Theses, 1517. Presbyterians brush past to get on to John Calvin at Geneva, 1536. Congregationalists are impatient lest the *Mayflower* should sail without them, 1620; while Baptists find an earlier beginning on the Continent, but in England are only a few years ahead. Quakers come down to George Fox and his inner light in 1646. Methodists must travel another hundred years to John Wesley and his warmed heart, 1738. That which Richard Hooker criticized in the Puritans of Elizabethan England may not be true of their descendants' faith, but it is still implied by much of their conduct:

' Ye plainly hold, that from the very Apostles' time till this present age, wherein yourselves imagine ye have found a right pattern of sound discipline, there never was any time safe to be followed.'[1]

We act as though, after the first heroic centuries, nothing of great import happened till our denominational re-beginnings of Church History.

In my garden is an ancient oak. It is always making dead wood, and I suppose it always has done. Some of it comes rattling down when the winds are blowing. Some of it last winter I felt that I must hack away—not without scars and gashes, for I am a clumsy though well-meaning woodsman. But whatever has gone wrong, I have never been tempted to single out one branch because it seemed to me the fairest foliage, and pretend that that was the tree. No, my favourite stem comes out of one of the main boughs, and that reaches down to the gnarled old trunk, and that disappears into the massive roots, and they reach down under the very spot where the first small acorn fell when it all began, a hundred and more years ago.

If Anglicans are omitted from the list of complaints

---

[1] *Laws of Ecclesiastical Polity*, preface iv, 2.

above, that is not because their theological education is faultless. Their fault, however, is other than lack of emphasis upon a *succession*. You would notice that the stout protagonist of the Elizabethan Settlement, Jewel, Bishop of Salisbury, while he rejects the current Roman notion of the succession of bishops in a see as something too mechanical, holds on to the idea of a succession—doctrinal succession. When in the Anglican Revival the Church of England began to transcend its long subordination to the State, it was from the historic succession that the writer of the first *Tract for the Times* in 1833, made his start:

' The Christian Ministry is a succession. And if we trace back the power of ordination from hand to hand, of course we shall come to the Apostles at last. We know we do as a plain historical fact: and therefore all we who have been ordained clergy, in the very form of our ordination, acknowledged the doctrine of the Apostolical Succession.'[1]

Ah, there it is! In spite of all our precautions we have not been able to keep those words from coming together. What shall we say about apostolic succession?

I feel about it much as I do about evolution, and I am as grateful to the Tractarians as I am to their contemporaries, the biologists. I agree with them just about as much. When Darwin and Spencer burst with their new theories upon a surprised world, they were so new that some thought that the whole thing was settled. Others were equally sure that the whole

---

[1] Newman. Convenient selections from the *Tracts* may be found in W. G. Hutchinson, *The Oxford Movement*; this on p. 9.

thing was damned—and that their fathers had been
wrong in thinking either the Pope or Napoleon to
be the Man of Sin—it was Darwin. You remember
Disraeli in 1864 rising in a diocesan conference which
was discussing the matter:

'In answer to the question, Is man an ape or an
angel? I, my Lord, am on the side of the angels.'[1]

So are we all. Yet we have accepted the revolution
in the natural sciences which Darwin began. Nor is
it science alone which is affected. The wider implications of the change are that every organism is an
historical being, to be understood in the light of its
history. That has changed Biblical study, Theology,
Sociology, Ethics, everything—and nothing more than
History in all its branches. We are not Darwinians.
Especially do we reject any mechanical interpretation
of the world of nature and man's emergence in it.
We accept the idea of a succession, but in a wider
context than the pioneers were capable of understanding.

Similarly with regard to the Oxford Movement:
whether your interpretation of history is the same as
Newman's ' plain historical fact ' or not, do acknowledge, I pray you, his valuable sense of historical
continuity, which is a fact, and one of the greatest
of facts. Let us be sure that it is there, just as sure
as that the evolutionary principle is there, influencing
our every subject.

If it is instructive to compare Tractarian and
Biologist in their emphasis upon continuity, it is also

[1] Quoted by F. S. Marvin, *Century of Hope*, p. 216.

necessary to compare the two religious revivals in the English Church, that in the eighteenth and that in the nineteenth century, in order to assess the extent of their influence. In both cases I always picture the ' movement ' as threefold: (1) a central splash, (2) a wider circle of disturbance, and (3) a ripple which goes out in all directions to the very margin of the stream. In the eighteenth-century revival the central splash is Methodism, in the nineteenth Anglo-Catholicism. A group of high-churchmen at Oxford University happens to be the reason for both. The second is happier than the first in one respect: a breach with their mother-church is felt to be neces-sary only by a few individuals, who go over to Rome; there is no secession on any large scale.

The wider circle of disturbance in the eighteenth century is Evangelicalism: the whole Church of England is affected by those who, while they do not follow the same methods as the Wesleys (itinerant preaching), nor accept the same theology (Arminian-ism), have come into the same living religious experi-ence. While the number of such clergy is not large, their lay following is influential, and by the end of the century they have already become ' the dominant religious power '.[1] Similarly the nineteenth-century movement changes the whole Church, not just one party within it. It uplifts the conception of the Church: Erastianism, if not destroyed, is doomed; henceforth it is the Church which matters, not its State connexion. The bishop is no more thought of as a figure in society but as a father-in-God; a clergy-

[1] Overton, *The Evangelical Revival in the Eighteenth Century*, p. 160.

man's is neither a career nor a living, but a cure of
souls.

It is the ripple which so many overlook. With
regard to the eighteenth-century revival, here is an
estimate of the widest extent of its influence:

' At a time when Bishop Butler asserted that Christianity was wearing out of the minds of men, Wesley kept
the English people Christian. . . . It is certain that into
the moral fibre of the English people, even in the classes
most anxious to repudiate the debt, were woven new
strands by the abiding influence of Methodism.'[1]

Because of the new power of religion in our land,
religious men are able to abolish slavery, start popular
education, begin prison reform, attack the evils of
woman- and child-labour. Above all, there comes to
all our churches the Missionary Awakening which is
the greatest event in modern history.

What is there to compare with this in the nineteenth-century revival? Denominations distant from
most of the positions of the Anglican Reformers here
too may be ' anxious to repudiate the debt ', or at
least may overlook it. Here is a judgment which may
stand as typical of such:

' The nature of their own principles drove some of the
leaders from that Church in the years that followed.
Those who remained were to influence it profoundly.
By their zeal and devotion they increased its vitality,
extended its influence . . . and strengthened the barriers
which separate it from non-episcopal churches.'

That last sentence shows only a partial understanding.

[1] Sir Charles Grant Robertson in Sir Charles Oman, *History of England*, Vol. IV, p. 386.

The fact is that the ripple has long since flowed beyond the circle of the Anglican communion, to affect the Church-consciousness of us all, revive our sense of continuity, exalt our churchmanship, and stir us with concern that the Church should come to worthier visible expression. Here it is that the two streams meet: viewed from the practical side, the cause of Church reunion owes most to the modern missionary movement. It is that which has carried us beyond the narrow environments where our divisions began and where they may still appear to belong. It is that which has brought us together by the pressure of a common need. Viewed in respect of attitude of mind and faith of heart, the cause of Church reunion equally depends upon this new churchmanship. Historically the first is connected with Methodist and Evangelical Revivals of the eighteenth century. The second is no less connected with the Anglican Revival of the nineteenth. Let us acknowledge our debt.

Succession: the Church is all ours, from the day when God called Abraham and 'he went out not knowing whither he went . . . for he looked for the City which hath the foundations . . .' to the day when we see 'the holy City, New Jerusalem, coming down out of heaven from God'. We are heirs of all the ages—*all*. We must teach and preach and live as being nothing less.

The second point is comprehension—which is near the original meaning of that misused word 'catholic'. I described in Chapter VIII how service in the Church overseas sometimes brings men—brought me at any rate—to this. If one's upbringing is in a communion belonging to the sect-ideal, the Church saved out of the world, much modern missionary service belongs to a strangely different environment. Here again in the wider life of the World-Church, one sees the impoverishment which we suffer by our divisions. It is this matter of 'either . . . or' which is so fatal. The rising generation must be introduced to a churchmanship wide enough to include diversities which in the past have caused division, developed enough to be a synthesis of lines of expression which before have been parallel, and, like all parallels, have not met. I have already quoted Polybius' saying about there being 'no more ready corrective of conduct than knowledge of the past'. Let us take two illustrations from the past that we may correct our conduct with regard to comprehension of this kind.

The first is the rise of Islam in the seventh century —the Church's grimmest crisis, and in some ways its first big defeat.

We have already compared the German invasions of the West in the fifth century, with the Arab outpouring in the East in the seventh. The Western invaders were influenced by the civilization of their neighbours, and, among other 'Roman' ways, those who lived on or near the frontiers began to adopt the Christian religion.[1] Is there anything to compare with this in the East? The Arabs were surrounded by potential Christian influences. North-east lay what is now Iraq, where the Church of the East (Nestorian) was strongest, with its Catholicos ruling from the Persian capital, Seleucia-Ctesiphon. To the north-west lay Syria, which was the eastern boundary

[1] Though in its Arian form.

of the Christian Empire. Many divisions troubled the Church here, Nestorian and Monophysite both. And more significant than the theological names of the parties was a disaffection to the Church of the Empire and a spirit of local independence. West lay Egypt and the African shore of the Red Sea. Egypt's Church (Coptic) had already pushed south, and Abyssinia was counted a Christian country. Moreover this Church had, with migrating traders and colonists, established itself on the southernmost tip of Arabia, the Yemen. North-east, north-west, west and south— encirclement by potential Christian influences was almost complete.

The nomads of the desert were as much a matter of suspicion to the settled empires of that day as the wild men beyond the Khyber Pass are to the Government of India. In a similar way those empires, both Roman and Persian, made use of friendly Arab tribes, subsidizing them to act as wardens of the marches. We may compare with these the many Goths who were accepted into the military service of the Western Empire. Among these Arab frontier tribes under foreign employ were to be found many Christians, especially in the north-west, i.e. those serving the Christian Empire.

In Arabia itself the old deities, crude conceptions of a primitive people, had lost their hold. On the positive side we may mark[1] in the poetry of the pre-Islamic period expressions of deep inner yearning for some better way; of consciousness of sin and God's coming judgment upon it—sin which is written down in God's book of knowledge; of sighing for forgive-

[1] R. Bell, *The Origin of Islam in its Christian Environment*.

ness and peace and heaven. Words of Syriac origin
seem to have been in common Arab use—and remember that it is only as an ecclesiastical language
that Syriac has become literary. Among these words
is the very word *Koran*—used in the Church of the
East for the reading of the lesson. Whether the still
more important word *Allah* (Syriac *Alaha*) is of such
a borrowing is a matter for debate by Semitic scholars.
It can hardly be doubted that much which is ascribed to Allah had come into Arab thought by way
of the monotheistic religions. Compared with these
borrowed religious conceptions, the old superstitions
were dying.

Within Mohammed's own family circle, the influence of Christianity was strong. Zeid, the slave of
Khadija, who was adopted as son by Mohammed,
was the child of Syrian Christian parents, stolen away
by marauding Arabs.[1] It makes one recall what happened to those marauding Goths who stole Christian
slaves from Cappadocia about the year 264, and
carried them over the Bosphorus.

'These pious captives, by their intercourse with the
barbarians, brought over large numbers to the true faith.
. . . Of the number of these captives were the ancestors
of Ulfilas himself '[2]

—the Ulfilas who became missionary, bishop, and
civilizer of the Goth (*c.* 341). The influence of Christian slaves was one of the means whereby God
prepared for the survival of His Church in the

[1] Muir, *The Life of Mohammad*, p. 34.
[2] Philostorgius, *Ecclesiastical History*, II, 5. Philostorgius was
contemporary with Ulfilas and himself a Cappadocian.

West when the invaders had brought the Empire to destruction. Was the same to be true in the East?

Bell begins his book with these words:

'From one point of view the triumph of Islam in the East . . . may be regarded as the judgment of history upon a degenerate Christianity.'[1]

Cash says:

'Christianity failed . . . to grip the Arab mind because of its schisms and divisions, and Mohammed in his study of Christianity reflects in the Koran all the errors of the day, the misconceptions of our faith, and the theological controversies.'[2]

He illustrates this from Mohammed's misunderstanding of baptism—the dyeing of Christians' clothes; of the Eucharist—a table come down from heaven by Christ's wonder-working; the Trinity—God, Jesus, and the Virgin Mary.

Muir adds this more positive statement:

'Had Mohammed witnessed a purer exhibition of the rites and doctrines (of the Church) and seen more of its reforming and regenerating influences, we cannot doubt that, in the sincerity of his early search after truth, he might readily have embraced and faithfully adhered to the faith of Jesus.'[3]

I cannot read the story without thinking of another movement, which since 1917 has swept across the world with the zeal of a new and aggressive religion.

[1] *The Origin of Islam*, p. 1.
[2] *Christendom and Islam*, p. 29.
[3] *The Life of Mohammad*, p. 21.

It has wiped out the Christian history of a stretch of the world's surface which lies parallel, on a more northerly latitude, to that of Islam's advance. From the frontier of what used to be Poland to within the north-west territories of China, Bolshevism has triumphed. When one considers some of its nobilities, its indignation at long-standing wrongs, its pity for the poor, the readiness it imparts to some of its young converts to endure hardship and even martyrdom, one can hardly doubt where this movement ought to have belonged. As the findings of the Madras Conference declare:

'When leaders of these movements (new paganisms) have turned against the Christian faith it has often been because many of the aspirations which stir them most deeply, though Christian in character, have been forgotten or suppressed by the Church. This fact should call Christians everywhere to penitence, and to a determined effort to apply the teachings of Christ to every area of life.'[1]

The Church shared in the oppression, and, itself corrupt, was partner with a corrupt State in continuing the exploitation of the poor. Our faith was misunderstood, and continues to be misrepresented. Christianity has found a new rival, and a terrible one, one which is a world power, claiming not less than the Church to have a universal message.

In the post-war world, with Russia our partner in victory over the great anti-Christ, will this other anti-Christian ideology have a more certain trumpet than we can find to sound? What troubles me most in

[1] *The Authority of the Faith*, Tambaram Madras Series, Vol. I, p. 209.

prospect of that event is that already there are those who call themselves ' Christian Communists '. Just as disaffected Christians of the eastern Mediterranean in the seventh century were foolish enough to welcome the Moslem invader, so some of these to-day whose Christian ideals may be strong but whose attachment to corporate Christianity is weak, talk as if concern for social uplift, a juster society, a true internationalism, were a tie which mattered more than the differences between religion and irreligion, love of God and godlessness, Christ and anti-Christ. They are the diffused idealists, who know something of Christ as He preached on the Mount, but have not seen the Church which is His Body.

But if we are faithful in this regard, I have a hope. In the Madras report there is one section called *The Unfinished Evangelistic Task.* A large part of the message of this book has been that the Universal Church has arrived—our Lord's purposes have for the first time come to anything like fulfilment—' the fulness of Him who is being out-and-out fulfilled '. I believe that that is a message, perhaps *the* message, for God's people in these days of depression and almost despair. But here is a different picture which is also true:

' Many countries or areas are entirely closed to Christian witness; among them are Afghanistan, the Soviet Republics, Bhutan, Outer Mongolia, Nepal, Tibet. The fact that countries once open are closing to the Gospel is a significant feature of our time. Missionaries in Turkestan have been driven out.'

Look at it on the map. Bolshevism accounts for most

M

of that greatest closed area of the world's surface.
Where are the keys? Where, I ask you, is there
more chance of finding them, since common need
forced us into this strangest of alliances, where—but
in the Church of this land? Those who stand together
in the hour of need will assuredly influence each
other afterwards. Perhaps we are afraid of Russia's
influence because we are uncertain of the power of
our own. But who has that which is stronger? Keys?
'The gates of Hell shall not prevail. I will give unto
thee the keys of the Kingdom of Heaven.'

That promise is not made to the mere social-
gospeller. Says the wise Origen:

'If thou hast Peter's faith, thou art a rock like him; if
thou hast Peter's virtues, thou hast Peter's keys.'[1]

The diffused idealists will not do it; they do not
believe enough. Christianity as a disembodied influence would not long survive the passing of the
Body. Diffused idealism would soon be only a
fragrance on the breeze. Indeed it might be only a
smell.

Here comes the second illustration, to give us this
time not warning, but example:

'I have loved righteousness and hated iniquity; and
therefore I die in exile.'[2]

Such was Hildebrand's judgment upon his own life.
After the bitter struggle between Papal and Imperial

---

[1] *Commentary on St. Matthew's Gospel*, xvi, 18f.
[2] Psalm xlv. 7.   R. E. Prothero, *The Psalms in Human Life*.
p. 76.

powers, Rome lay in ruins, the Emperor Henry IV had set up his anti-Pope, and he, the Pope, was breathing his last in the castle of Salerno, in the year 1085. I want you to notice the idealism—for all the clash and strife, the underhand scheming, the shameless use of worldly weapons, do not lose sight of it: Hildebrand seeks to fulfil that deep religious conviction of loyal hearts everywhere, that Holy Church stands above the international anarchy, God's agent for the redemption of the world, the realization *in* the world of the eternal City of God. When in 410 Rome fell, and it was twilight in Western Europe, we saw this faith shine forth from Augustine with a brightness which was never forgotten. About 750, when the Dark Ages are really here, you may catch a glimpse of it again, though less noble in its expression: a forgery, not to be exposed for nearly seven hundred years, the *Donation of Constantine*, is set forth as a charter from the Emperor transferring Western sovereignty to the Pope. Its significance, unaffected by its falsehood, is that it is to the Church that idealists are turning in what would otherwise be a time of unrelieved despair. A century later, when the brief brightness of Charlemagne's Empire has passed, and darkness settles again over the land, we find a similar forgery, the *Isidorian Decretals*. In a Europe of hopeless division, men are looking to the Church and to the Vicar of Christ as the only possible unifying factor.

Hildebrand, in trying to bring these age-long aspirations to fulfilment, makes one advance on the highest doctrines of the Papacy yet set forward. Instead of the dual theocracy to which medieval

thought was by now accustomed, Pope and Emperor,
God's vice-regents, each in his own sphere—the modified descendant of St. Augustine's ' two cities '[1]—
Hildebrand claims that one power is supreme, the
Pope's. It is his ' to give and to take away, empires,
kingdoms, marquisates, duchies, countships, and the
possessions of all men '. To him is the ultimate
loyalty : ' He may absolve subjects from their fealty
to wicked men.' There is only one vice-regent, and
all other powers, even the Emperor, hold their rule
as vassals; their kingdoms are fiefs, given, or withheld, by the Pope.

The judgment of history upon him is that though
it was a magnificent ideal which he tried to realize,
that of the supra-national Church, making the dark,
divided, warring world into a real theocracy, he tried
to attain a religious end by playing on the statesman's
chessboard and using the world's pieces : he moved
his pawns there—the recalcitrant barons of Germany;
a castle here—the Countess Matilda's at Canossa; and
now his knights—Robert Guiscard and his Normans
from South Italy. He lost.

His successor, Pope Urban II, did not succeed to
his conflict. He was the Pope who launched the First
Crusade, and the cry resounded through Europe,
Deus vult. The Crusades have been called the first
popular movement of European history. They were
the first action of anything like a united Europe, transcending for the moment not only racial hatreds and
national jealousies, but also the feudal divisions within each nation. They were an augury of the possible
emergence of a united Christendom. In the first flush

[1] See pp. 25-27 above.

of enthusiasm men forgot the long-standing differences between Greek and Latin Churches. But what strikes me most is this judgment of a modern historian:

' On the flood of the crusading movement Urban rose at once to a position of European leadership. Henry IV and Wibert (anti-Pope) might oppose him, but the Papacy had *achieved a popular significance compared with which they had nothing to offer*.'[1]

What was it there that set me dreaming? We have seen the unfulfilment of a supra-national ideal—like Hildebrand's a worthy one and a Christian—in the League of Nations. This ideal rose for most of us like a beacon out of the long night through which we had come. It still glimmered, though with an ever more flickering light, against the divided nationalisms and international anarchy which since 1931 threatened us with the return of the Dark Ages. We were not to attain to a religious end by methods of the world's diplomacy. Perhaps in this greater darkness we may see again the Church as guiding star, the world-wide Church—which has surely come to pass—as object of our transcendent loyalty. Its authority nowadays we do not seek in the universal sway of any earthly pontiff. But by some movement big enough to appeal to all who call themselves Christian, the Church may again unite its scattered members, lift us above our national barriers, heal our denominational divisions, and, above all, achieve a popular significance compared with which the fallen Hitler and Mussolini,

[1] Williston Walker, *A History of the Christian Church*, p. 233. Italics are mine.

and even the victorious Stalin, might be seen to have had nothing to offer. Comprehension: that would be indeed the Church in the world, but a supra-mundane Church.

This book begins and ends with a plea for church-manship. I have made it because I believe that the Church *is* His Body, even the Church, with all its shortcomings, as it is among us.

'The Word made flesh': Creator of all things,
   Earth's myriad fruits, and ocean's mighty swell,
—He waits the food which a disciple brings,
   And thirsty, asks a woman at the well.

'The Church His Body': Thus, incarnate still,
   And bound by human weaknesses to-day,
He has no hands but ours to do His will,
   No feet but laggard ours to walk His way.

O Lord, Thou didst our limitations share
   From Thy conception in the Virgin's womb,
Through want and toil and loneliness and care,
   To death on cross, and burial in the tomb.

And now—Thy Church has failed, I hear men say:
   In every age disciples Thee forsake,
Peters deny and Judases betray.
   Yet help me love Thy Body for Thy sake.

The Church is His Body, and He is Head over all.

The last word which is to be spoken by any of us with regard to education for churchmanship cannot be far from that word of Martin Luther:

'The chief lesson and study of divinity is that we learn

well and rightly to know Christ, who is therein **very** graciously pictured forth unto us.'[1]

There we will end, because there is a question, about preparation of ourselves, or training of others, which matters most of all.

[1] *Luther's Table-Talk*, §182.

INDEX

ABYSSINIA, Church in, 47, 173
Africa, Church in, 36, 110, 154f., 156f.
Aidan, Bishop, 120, 156
Alopen, Bishop, 120
' American Christianity ', 148
Anglo-Saxons, Conversion of, 29, 63, 114-116, 120f., 156
Animism, behind both Roman and Japanese State cults, 94-96
Apocalyptic, 19, 89, 106, 136, 148
Apostolic Succession, 162-164, 167-171
Arabs, 47, 172-174
Arnold, Matthew, 130; of Rugby, 130
Augustine, Archbishop of Canterbury, 29, 63, 115f., 120, 156
Augustine, Bishop of Hippo, *De Civitate Dei*, 20-31, 34, 37, 151, 179f.; *Epistles*, 31; *Retractions*, 21

BAPTISM, 50, 68, 70f., 175
Baptists, 53, 127f., 153, 165f.
Bede, *Ecclesiastical History*, 115f., .120
Bell, Richard, *The Origin of Islam in its Christian Environment*, 173-175
Benedict, Saint, 63
Bible, Translation of, 32, 81, 118, 155f.; Critical study of, 79f., 134, 168
British Israelites, 95
Buddhism, 43, 49, 81, 91f., 118f.
Butler, Bishop, 170

Cambridge Modern History, 61f.
Canton, 50; Fall of (1938), 15
Carey, William, 127f., 153; *Life of*, by S. Pearce Carey, 153
Cash, W. Wilson, *Christendom and Islam*, 175
Celsus (Origen, *Contra Celsum*), 66, 77, 80, 87-89, 132f.
Chao, T. C., 110
China, 15, 17, 36-38, 43f., 87, 91; Church in, 38, 43-44, 50, 53, 55, 67f., 77-79, 107, 110, 112, 117-121, 153-155, 157
Church:
  buildings, 22f., 52, 71f., 112, 115f., 119n.; a refuge, from Goths, 22; from Japanese, 22f.
  central in Christianity, 20, 27f., 33, 39, 148-152
  central in history, 26f., 39f., 61f.
  doctrine concerning the, 27f., 32-35, 111, 122f., 130f., 141-183. *And see* Kingdom of God and Church

Church—*continued*
  of England, 45, 55f., 163, 166-171
  of the West, in the early centuries, 66-83, 87-89, 96f., 99-103, 106-109, 142f.
  in the Middle Ages, 45, 47, 55, 61, 63, 114, 143-146, 153, 156-158, 178-181
  of Scotland, 11f., 64, 128, 147
  of other countries. *See under* country
  reunion, 41-58, 160f., 170f.
  and State, in Roman Empire (pagan), 84-103; (Christian), 27, 29-32, 143f.
    in medieval Europe, 178-181
    in England, 45, 53, 167, 169; in Scotland, 147
    in Russia, 176; in Japanese Empire, 84-103; in China, 77, 157
  Unity of, 34, 42, 52, 56, 58, 157f., 162f., 166
  Universality of, 90, 119-123, 130f., 162, 177; in New Testament, 38, 107; in St. Augustine, 34; at Madras Conference, 34, 39f., 42, 111
Church History, Teaching of, 11, 20, 122, 132, 136-140, 152, 165, 168
Chrysostom, Saint John, *Homilies on the Epistle to the Romans*, 31
City of God, *De Civitate Dei*. *See* Augustine
Collective security, 16, 57, 181
Comity in missionary work, 51, 56
Communion. *See* Eucharist
Communism, 16f., 36, 50, 79, 149, 175-178
Confucianism, 110, 118
Congregationalism, 44-46, 53, 147, 155, 157, 159, 165
Constantine, Emperor, 29, 143; *Donation of*, 179; a Chinese, 77
Co-operation in missionary work, 50f., 56, 153n.
Coptic Church, 47, 173
Crusades, 180
Cyprian, Bishop of Carthage, *De Lapsis*, 144

DARK AGES, 20, 27, 29, 36, 63, 144, 155, 179, 181
Darwin, Charles, 167f.
Devolution, from Mission to Church, 53
Didache, 67-75
Disraeli, Benjamin, 168

185

QUOTATIONS FROM OR REFERENCES TO SCRIPTURE

Page numbers are given in italics

QUOTATIONS FROM HISTORICAL DOCUMENTS

**Books are to be returned on or before
the last date below**